Blackstone Griddle Secrets

Elevate Your Cooking Skills with Precision Temperature Control, 2000+ Flavorful Recipes and Essential Maintenance - Your Ultimate Journey to Culinary Excellence

Dr. Alfred Bennett

Table of Content:

Introduction

Unleashing Your Blackstone Potential

Welcome to the enriching world of griddle cooking, where your new Blackstone Griddle is not just a cooking tool, but a gateway to expanding your culinary prowess. This section is designed not just to motivate but to empower you, sharpen your skills, and help you tap into the vast capabilities of your griddle.

Exploring the Core of Griddling

At its core, griddling is about precision and connection—the precise heat application on durable metal and the unique ways flavors bond on its surface. When you use your Blackstone, you're set to manipulate these elements expertly. This griddle turns a simple cooking routine into a dynamic way to prepare delicious meals, making every occasion special and every meal a memory.

Simplifying the Process

It's common to feel a bit unsure when you first encounter a professional tool like the Blackstone Griddle. However, this feeling quickly dissipates with proper guidance and practice. Here, we strip away the complexity that surrounds professional cooking equipment. Each chapter is built to gradually enhance your comfort and confidence, ensuring that what seemed intricate becomes straightforward through consistent practice and clear instructions.

Adopting Expert Techniques

Achieving mastery over your griddle is a realistic goal. This book offers detailed yet easy-to-follow advice that demystifies the sophisticated techniques used by professional chefs. By engaging with each section, you will learn how to effectively control your griddle, mastering everything from delicate pancakes to sumptuous steaks, without the frustration.

Integrating the Griddle into Daily Use

Think of your Blackstone Griddle as more than a cooking device—it's a part of your daily life, a means to feed your passion for cooking and sharing meals. Each guideline and recipe here aims to make your griddle indispensable, simplifying meal preparation whether you're cooking for two or entertaining a crowd.

Transforming Everyday Meals

With your griddle, everyday ingredients transform into extraordinary meals. Understand how to exploit its surface for both slow cooking and searing, which unveils robust flavors and textures that typical cooking methods can't match. The griddles' expansive surface accommodates multiple foods at once, reducing cooking time and creating harmonious dishes that delight the palate.

Laying the Groundwork for Continued Innovation

This book serves as both a beginning and a foundation for ongoing culinary development. With every chapter, you build solid griddling skills that encourage future experimentation and creativity. We start with essential techniques and recipes, setting you up for advanced griddling adventures that promise to engage and challenge you.

<u>Bonus</u>

Before you dive into the wealth of knowledge this book offers about mastering your Blackstone Griddle, I'd like to draw your attention to an exclusive bonus that serves as a perfect complement to this guide. Titled '10 Pitfalls to Avoid with Your Blackstone Griddle', this bonus material is designed to broaden your understanding by delineating crucial do's and don'ts. These insights aim to optimize your griddle use, ensuring you evade common mistakes that even seasoned griddlers can make.

This additional resource promises to refine your techniques and elevate your griddling to expert levels. Consider it an essential sidekick to the main content of this book, filling in any gaps and reinforcing key concepts to transform your outdoor cooking experience fully.

To access this invaluable bonus for free, simply scan the QR code provided in the back of this book. Equip yourself with this enhanced knowledge and ensure a smooth, enjoyable griddle journey.

Chapter 1:

Understanding Your Blackstone Griddle

1.1 The Basics of Blackstone Griddles

Understanding The Blackstone Griddle

Imagine a canvas where your culinary dreams take shape, brought to life by the sizzle of premium cuts, the aroma of fresh spices, and the vibrant colors of crisp vegetables. This canvas is none other than the Blackstone Griddle. Crafted from cold-rolled steel, the griddle's surface offers a generous cooking area, enabling you to prepare multiple dishes simultaneously, a crucial feature for those bustling family gatherings or weekend cookouts.

Designed with versatility in mind, your Blackstone can accompany you through the crack of dawn with pancakes and bacon, find its stride doing midday burgers and hot dogs, and elegantly dance into the evening with seared steaks or a medley of sautéed vegetables. The essence of the Blackstone lies in its ability to cater to any meal, any craving, at any time.

The Heartbeat of Your Griddle: The Burners

Beneath the robust steel surface of your griddle lies the heartbeat of the Blackstone: its burners. Typically boasting two to four independent burners (depending on the model), these are what render the Blackstone a powerhouse of culinary versatility. Each burner can be controlled separately, providing you with the flexibility to create distinct cooking zones. A zone can be a searing hot surface perfect for steaks on one end, while the other could be a lower, gentler heat ideal for cooking vegetables or warming buns.

The independence of these burners invites an approach to cooking that is both art and science—allowing for creativity and precision in equal measure. It requires understanding and respect for the food being cooked and the heat it requires.

Navigating the Fuel Source

Your Blackstone Griddle operates on propane gas, a clean, efficient fuel that ensures consistent heat and immediate cooking action—there's no long wait for the griddle to reach the right temperature. Moreover, the ease with which propane tanks can be connected and replaced makes the Blackstone a reliable companion for both backyard cookouts and remote camping trips alike.

The Rite of Passage: Seasoning Your Griddle

While touched on lightly here and expanded upon in later chapters, it's essential to mention the crucial initial step of seasoning your griddle. This process not only protects your griddle's surface but also creates a non-stick patina that enriches the flavor of every dish that kisses its surface. Seasoning transforms your griddle from a mere cooking apparatus into a living chronicle of your culinary exploits.

1.2 Initial Unboxing and Assembly

Welcome to the first real step in your Blackstone Griddle experience! Unpacking and assembling your new griddle isn't just about putting pieces together; it's the first tangible moment of transforming your outdoor cooking into something truly special. This process, when done with care and attention, ensures a foundation for safe, enjoyable, and efficient cooking sessions. Let's guide you through it step by step.

Unpacking Your Blackstone Griddle

As you slice through the packing tape and peel back the cardboard flaps, you'll find several components neatly arranged. You have the main griddle top, the frame which includes legs and shelves, a grease management system, and various hardware like screws and knobs. Each of these plays a vital role in the assembly and functionality of your griddle.

Start by identifying and laying out all the parts. It's wise to ensure everything listed in the manual is present. Check for any transportation damages that might have occurred, though rare, it's better to address them before assembly.

Setting up the Base Frame

The base frame is like the backbone of your griddle. Depending on your specific Blackstone model, the base frame assembly might vary slightly, but the fundamental steps remain consistent. Begin by attaching the legs to the lower frame using the provided bolts and nuts. These should fit snugly; a loose frame can cause instability during cooking. Once the legs are secured, attach the side and bottom shelves. These not only provide structural support but also offer convenient storage and prep spaces.

On some models, you might find wheels or casters. Attach these as per the instructions, ensuring they're tight and locked into place. A mobile griddle means you can effortlessly move your cooking station to suit the sun, shade, or shelter, enhancing your overall outdoor culinary experience.

Installing the Griddle Top

The griddle top is the heart of your cooking station. It's usually heavy, so it's prudent to have an extra pair of hands to help lift and place it securely on the base frame. Make sure that the surface sits evenly on all sides. This is crucial for uniform heating during cooking.

Once in position, fasten any additional screws or bolts that connect the griddle top to the frame. This secures the top, preventing any movement as you cook. It's important to note that some model's design allows for slight expansion and contraction of the griddle top due to heat, so follow the specified instructions regarding how tight these connections should be.

Hooking up the Propane and Testing the Ignition

Safety first, always! Connecting the propane tank is a straightforward process but requires careful attention to detail. Ensure all burner knobs are in the 'OFF' position. Connect the regulator hose to the propane tank and tighten by hand. No tools are necessary here, as over-tightening can damage the regulator.

Once securely connected, slowly open the valve on your propane tank and check for any signs of leaks. A simple soapy water solution applied around the connection points will bubble up if there's a leak. If you discover a leak, shut off the gas immediately, disconnect, and retry connecting, ensuring everything is aligned and sealed correctly.

With everything connected and checked, turn one burner knob to 'IGNITE' and press the igniter. You should hear a clicking sound followed by the whoosh of the burner lighting. Repeat this for all burners to ensure they are all functioning correctly.

Final Steps Before Cooking

With the griddle assembled and burners tested, there are just a few more touches. Place the grease tray or cup in its designated spot to catch oil and food residues during cooking. This makes cleaning up afterward much simpler. Also, attach any additional accessories like side trays or utensil hooks that come with your model. These enhance your cooking experience by keeping everything you need within arm's reach.

1.3: Seasoning Your Griddle for the First Time

The Why and the What of Seasoning

The very essence of seasoning lies in its twofold benefit—protection and performance. The process involves coating your griddle top with a thin layer of oil, which, when heated, polymerizes. This means the oil undergoes a chemical transformation to create a hard, protective layer that guards against rust and creates a naturally non-stick surface. Not all oils are created equal for this task. What you seek is an oil with a high smoke point—the temperature at which an oil starts to break down and smoke. Canola, flaxseed, and grapeseed oil stand out as prime candidates, with high smoke points that suit the high heat of seasoning perfectly.

The Crucible of Seasoning: Phase One

Setting the stage for seasoning requires a clean slate. Begin with your griddle assembled and connected to the gas supply, as outlined in chapter 1.2. Ensure the griddle top is free of any manufacturing debris, dust, or protective coating. A little soapy water and a scouring pad should suffice for this initial wash. Rinse thoroughly with water and dry it off completely with cloth or paper towels.

Now, fire up your Blackstone Griddle on a low setting for about 15 minutes so that it's warm to the touch but not too hot to handle. It's essential that you get this right—the warmth will open the pores of the metal, readying the surface to bond with the oil.

The Crucible of Seasoning: Phase Two

Armed with your chosen oil and some paper towels or a high heat-resistant brush, apply a very thin layer of oil over the entire surface of the griddle. Aim for a sheen without any excess puddles. With the layer applied, crank up the heat to high, and let the magic begin. You're looking for the oil to start smoking and the griddle color to begin changing to a darker, bronzed hue.

This is not a time for impatience; the oil needs to smoke off completely, leaving behind the hardened, protective coat. This process may take 30 minutes or so, and proper ventilation is crucial—outdoor seasoning is preferable not only for the ample space but also for that intangible quality the great outdoors imparts.

The Crucible of Seasoning: Phase Three

Once the smoke dissipates and the griddle looks dark and dry, turn off the heat. Let it cool down a bit—enough so you can safely maneuver for another oiling cycle. This stage is vital: your griddle's resilience and non-stick quality build with every layer, so at least three layers are recommended for an armor-like finish. Repeat the oiling and heating process, watching as your griddle takes on a darker color with each round, signaling the maturity of the seasoning.

The Conductor's Baton—Managing Heat

Throughout the process, your attention to the temperature is non-negotiable. Too hot too fast and the oil could reach its smoke point prematurely without adequately bonding to the metal. Too cool, and the oil remains a sticky, tacky mess, a prime surface for food to latch onto instead of gliding off gracefully.

Beyond the First Base Layer

Your initial seasoning forms the bedrock for your griddle's performance, yet maintenance seasoning, will ensure your griddle's surface remains at its non-stick peak.After each cooking session, once the griddle cools down, consider wiping a thin layer of oil to maintain the integrity of the seasoning.

First Cook

With your griddle seasoned, the stage is set for your inaugural cooking performance. This maiden voyage into the world of Blackstone griddling should start with something simple and forgiving—vegetables with forgiving cook times or a batch of bacon that adds to the seasoning with its own fats.

Let your griddle cool down completely before you embark on your first culinary creation. Remember, the oils embedded in the seasoning are your allies, ensuring that tantalizing flavors are delivered and a pure, wholesome taste experience is preserved.

1.4: Griddle Accessories and Utensils

Recognizing the right tools will not only simplify your cooking process but will significantly enhance the outcome of your culinary endeavors.

The Essential Trio: Spatula, Scraper, and Tongs

At the heart of griddle cooking are three indispensable tools: the spatula, scraper, and tongs. Each serves a unique purpose that, when utilized properly, streamlines your cooking process, ensuring delectable results with every meal.

The Spatula: Opting for a high-quality, sturdy spatula will make flipping burgers, turning pancakes, and maneuvering delicate fish remarkably smooth. The broad, flat surface offers ample support to your foods, minimizing the risk of them falling apart as you lift. This tool is your primary interaction with the food, making its design—preferably with an ergonomic handle and heat resistance—a crucial aspect to consider.

The Scraper: Post-cooking cleanup is where the scraper shines. Designed to remove burnt-on food residue and grease, an efficient scraper keeps your griddle surface clean and well-maintained, ready for its next use. It's not just about cleanliness; a smooth surface ensures even cooking and flavor consistency across dishes.

Tongs: When handling vegetables or meats, a pair of tongs becomes an extension of your hand. It allows for quick, precise movements, flipping steaks or mixing grilled veggies without disturbing their cooking process. Tongs offer safety, keeping your hands at a distance from the hot griddle surface while providing the agility needed for efficient food management.

Basting Covers: Are you aiming for that perfect cheese melt on your burger? Or perhaps, a tender, steam-cooked vegetable medley? The basting cover is your ally. By trapping heat, it speeds up cooking times and ensures even heat distribution, crucial for melting and steaming without drying out the food.

Thermometers: An instant-read thermometer removes the guesswork from cooking meats. Safety and doneness are paramount when it comes to proteins like chicken, pork, and beef. With a thermometer, you can ensure each piece reaches the ideal internal temperature, guaranteeing both safety and perfect texture.

Squeeze Bottles: Efficiency and precision in oiling your griddle or applying sauces to your dishes can make a significant difference. Squeeze bottles enable controlled distribution, ensuring your griddle is properly conditioned for non-stick cooking and your food is evenly flavored.

Basting Brushes: Whether it's applying a delicate glaze to barbecued ribs or buttering your morning pancakes, a basting brush is essential for spreading liquids evenly over your cooking surface or food. Opt for silicone brushes for their durability and ease of cleaning.

Chapter 2:

Temperature Mastery

2.1 Understanding Heat Distribution

Mastering the art of griddle cooking begins with an intimate understanding of one of its most foundational elements: heat distribution. This isn't simply about turning the burners on and off. It's about recognizing how heat behaves on your Blackstone Griddle's surface, how it affects different foods, and how you can harness this knowledge to achieve culinary perfection with each dish you prepare.

The Art and Science of Heat

Heat distribution on a griddle isn't uniform; it varies across the surface, offering different cooking zones—hot, medium, and warm. This disparity is due to the placement of the burners beneath the griddle plate and the material properties of the griddle surface. The areas directly above the burners will be the hottest, ideal for searing and browning. As you move away from these points, the temperature gradually decreases, allowing for slower cooking processes.

Understanding this gradient is crucial. It enables you to cook multiple components of your meal simultaneously, but at their respective ideal temperatures. For instance, while searing a steak in the hottest zone, you can gently sauté vegetables or toast buns in the cooler areas. Mastering this art ensures each element of your meal is cooked perfectly and ready to serve at the same time.

The Material Matters

The material of your Blackstone Griddle plays a significant role in how heat is distributed and retained. Cast iron, renowned for its excellent heat retention and even heating after being fully warmed up, is a common material for these griddles. Initially, there may be slight differences in temperature across the surface, but with continued heating, cast iron distributes the heat more evenly, creating a versatile cooking surface. This characteristic makes the griddle incredibly efficient for a variety of cooking techniques, from searing at high temperatures to cooking delicate items that require a gentle heat. Knowing how to manage the initial heat up and understanding your griddle's specific heat retention properties will dramatically enhance your cooking experience.

Managing Heat - Beyond the Knobs

Adjusting the temperature isn't just about twisting the knobs to set the burners to high, medium, or low. It's about the strategic placement of food on the griddle surface, managing the lid (if your model includes one) to control the ambient temperature, and even using external elements like the wind to your advantage in outdoor settings. For example, opening the lid or removing a cover can introduce cooler air to the cooking space, slightly reducing the temperature. This can be a useful technique when your griddle gets too hot and your food begins to cook faster than anticipated. Conversely, closing the lid will trap heat within, creating an oven-like environment that's ideal for roasting or baking.

Practice Makes Perfect

The final, and perhaps most important, aspect of mastering heat distribution on your Blackstone Griddle is practice. Each griddle behaves slightly differently due to material variances, usage patterns, and even the external environment. Start with simple meals to get a feel for how your griddle heats up and cools down. Pay attention to how different foods react when placed in various zones on the griddle.

Consider keeping a cooking diary, noting what worked and what didn't, the settings used, and the outside temperature and weather conditions, if applicable. Overtime, you'll build a robust understanding of how to control the heat effectively, making adjustments intuitively based on what you're cooking.

2.2 Controlling Temperature for Different Foods

The Heat Each Food Deserves

Let's start with the basics: not all foods are created equal when it comes to the heat required for cooking. For example, a thick, juicy steak needs a high and intense heat to achieve that perfect sear on the outside while keeping the inside tender and moist. On the other hand, something more delicate, like eggs or pancakes, calls for a gentler, even heat.

To handle this diverse range of needs, your Blackstone Griddle offers incredible versatility with its multiple heating zones. You can have one area cranked up to high for searing meats, while another might be set on low to gently cook toppings or side dishes. The beauty of this setup is that it allows you to prepare disparate components of your meal simultaneously, ensuring everything comes off the griddle at the same time, ready to serve.

Temperature Tactics for Meats

Cooking meats on your Blackstone Griddle is an art that balances time and temperature. Take, for instance, beef. Depending on the cut and preference for doneness, the temperature can vary significantly. A rule of thumb is hot and fast for steaks, medium for burgers to ensure they are cooked through without burning the exterior, and low and slow for larger cuts like brisket that benefit from a more extended cooking period to break down the fibers and tenderize.

Chicken, prone to drying out if overcooked, requires a medium-high heat that seals in juices swiftly and then a medium-low environment to finish cooking without becoming too tough. Pork chops, like steaks, thrive under higher heat initially to create a savory crust.

Seafood and Heat: A Delicate Dance

Seafood asks for a sensitive approach. Shrimp and scallops, for example, are best cooked quickly over high heat to prevent them from becoming rubbery. Thicker fish fillets like salmon can handle medium-high heat, which gives the skin time to crisp up without overcooking the delicate flesh inside.

Vegetables and Fruits

Vegetables and fruits on the griddle are a revelation but remember that different types call for varying heat levels. Dense vegetables like potatoes or carrots benefit from a medium heat that cooks them through without charring their outsides beyond recognition. Asparagus or bell peppers, being more tender, require a higher heat for a shorter time to achieve a pleasant char while maintaining a crisp texture.

Managing Temperature Fluctuations

One crucial aspect of temperature control is understanding how the Blackstone Griddle retains and radiates heat. The cast iron surface, once heated, tends to hold onto that heat, making it imperative to monitor and adjust the flame periodically actively. This is especially vital on windy days or when the external environment affects the griddle's temperature.

A practical approach to managing this is to start foods on a higher heat zone and then move them to a cooler area of the griddle to finish cooking. This technique is not just effective for managing doneness and texture but also allows you to free up space on hotter parts of the griddle for other items that need initial searing.

2.3: Using the Zones on Your Griddle

Mastering your Blackstone Griddle involves more than just firing it up and throwing on your food. It's about understanding how to effectively use the varied temperature zones to your advantage, creating a symphony of flavors and textures that elevate your outdoor cooking from simple to spectacular.

The Essentials of Zone Cooking

This feature allows you to cook multiple dishes at once, each requiring different cooking temperatures. Essentially, the griddle is divided into areas that can be set to high, medium, or low heat.

Heat Zones: Learning the Layout

Understanding the layout of your Blackstone Griddle is the first step toward effective zone usage. Typically, the zones nearest to the gas burners will be the hottest. As you move away from the burners, the temperature naturally decreases. This creates a gradient of heat across the griddle, from very hot to moderate to low, allowing for versatile cooking techniques and the ability to handle a variety of ingredients simultaneously.

Strategic Cooking: Hot Zone Techniques

In the hottest part of the griddle, you'll want to sear meats or cook items that require high temperatures for a crisp exterior. This zone is perfect for creating a delicious char on steaks, grilling burgers, or charring veggies for that extra flavor. The intense heat quickly sears the surface of the food, locking in flavors and juices.

Middle Management: Medium Zone Mastery

The medium zones are the versatile heart of the griddle. This is where most of the cooking happens. Foods that need a gentler touch or require thorough cooking without burning thrive here. You can perfectly cook chicken breasts, sauté onions until they're just translucent, or cook mouth-watering grilled sandwiches. It's also ideal for foods that need a shorter cooking time but are sensitive to extreme heat.

Low and Slow: The Cool Zone

The coolest part of the griddle is not to be underestimated. It's perfect for foods that need slow cooking or just keeping warm without further cooking. Think delicate fish, thinner vegetables like zucchini or bell peppers, or simply using it as a resting place for foods cooked on hotter parts of the griddle. It's also great for gently toasting buns or tortillas without scorching them.

Transitioning Between Zones

Mastering the movement of food between zones is a skill that comes with practice and is key to managing a full meal on the griddle. Start steaks on the hot part to get a good sear, then move them to a cooler zone to finish cooking internally without burning the outside. Similarly, pancakes can be started in a medium zone for browning and then shifted to a low area to stay warm while you finish cooking the rest of the batch.

Timing and Coordination

The real magic happens when you bring it all together. Cooking multiple items with different needs means you need to be adept at timing and coordination. Begin with foods that take the longest or can benefit from resting once cooked. Use the hotter zones for quick-cook items toward the end of your griddle session. Always be mindful of what each dish requires and anticipate where and when each piece of your culinary puzzle will fit on the griddle.

Griddle Zone Management: Cooking in Harmony

Becoming proficient with zone management on your Blackstone Griddle enhances not just the quality of the dishes you prepare but also the enjoyment and satisfaction of cooking outdoors. It allows you to smoothly orchestrate the creation of complex meals, handling everything from delicate items to hearty steaks with equal flair. This skill ensures that everything comes off the griddle at the optimum temperature, maximizing both flavor and texture.The underlying principle here is not to overpower but to harmonize; understanding the zones allows you to align the cooking needs of various ingredients seamlessly.

Chapter 3:

Breakfast Delights

3.1 Griddling the Perfect Pancake

Recipe 1: Classic Buttermilk Griddle Pancakes

Preparation time = 15 minutes

Ingredients = 2 cups all-purpose flour | 2 tablespoons granulated sugar | 1 teaspoon baking powder | 1 teaspoon baking soda | 1/2 teaspoon salt | 2 cups buttermilk | 1 teaspoon vanilla extract | 2 large eggs | 4 tablespoons unsalted butter, melted

Servings = Serves 4

Mode of cooking: Griddling

Procedure: In a large bowl, whisk together flour, sugar, baking powder, baking soda, and salt. In another bowl, blend buttermilk, vanilla extract, and eggs. Pour in the melted butter and mix well. Gently fold the wet ingredients into the dry mixture until few lumps remain. Be careful not to overmix as this can make the pancakes tough. Preheat your Blackstone Griddle to 375°F and lightly oil the surface. Pour 1/4 cup of batter for each pancake onto the griddle. Cook until the edges appear set and bubbles form on the surface, about 2-3 minutes. Flip the pancakes and cook for an additional 1-2 minutes on the other side until golden brown. Serve these classic pancakes hot with butter and maple syrup.

Nutritional values: Approx. 310 calories | 8g protein | 9g fats | 49g carbohydrates

---

Recipe 2: Banana Nut Griddle Pancakes

Preparation time = 15 minutes

Ingredients = 2 cups all-purpose flour | 1/4 cup brown sugar | 2 teaspoons baking powder | 1/2 teaspoon salt | 1 ripe banana, mashed | 1 1/2 cups milk | 1 egg | 3 tablespoons butter, melted | 1/2 cup chopped walnuts

Servings = Serves 4

Mode of cooking: Griddling

Procedure: Combine flour, brown sugar, baking powder, and salt in a large bowl.In another bowl, mix together the mashed banana, milk, egg, and melted butter.Add the wet ingredients to the dry ingredients and stir until just blended. Fold in the chopped walnuts.Preheat your Blackstone Griddle to 375°F. Grease with a light coating of butter or oil.Pour 1/4 cup of batter onto the griddle for each pancake. Cook until bubbles form on the surface and the edges are dry, around 2-3 minutes.Flip the pancakes carefully and cook for another 2 minutes or until golden brown.

Serve warm with a drizzle of honey or syrup.

Nutritional values: Approx. 340 calories | 9g protein | 14g fats | 51g carbohydrates

---

Recipe 3: Chocolate Chip Griddle Pancakes

Preparation time = 15 minutes

Ingredients = 2 cups all-purpose flour | 3 tablespoons sugar | 1 tablespoon baking powder | 1/2 teaspoon salt | 1 3/4 cups milk | 2 teaspoons vanilla extract | 2 large eggs | 4 tablespoons butter, melted | 1 cup semi-sweet chocolate chips

Servings = Serves 4

Mode of cooking: Griddling

Procedure: In a large bowl, mix together the flour, sugar, baking powder, and salt.Combine the milk, vanilla extract, and eggs in a separate bowl, then whisk in the melted butter.Pour the wet ingredients into the dry ingredients, stirring until just combined. Fold in the chocolate chips.Heat the Blackstone Griddle to 375°F and lightly grease the surface.Scoop 1/4 cup of pancake batter onto the griddle and cook until the surface starts to bubble, about 2 minutes.Flip the pancakes and cook until the other side is golden brown, about 1-2 minutes more.Serve hot with whipped cream or your favorite pancake topping.

Nutritional values: Approx. 395 calories | 9g protein | 18g fats | 55g carbohydrates

Recipe 4: Blueberry Lemon Griddle Pancakes

Preparation time = 15 minutes

Ingredients = 2 cups all-purpose flour | 1/4 cup sugar | 2 teaspoons baking powder | 1/2 teaspoon salt | Zest of 1 lemon | 2 cups milk | 2 eggs | 3 tablespoons butter, melted | 1 cup fresh blueberries

Servings = Serves 4

Mode of cooking: Griddling

Procedure: Mix the flour, sugar, baking powder, salt, and lemon zest in a large bowl.In a separate bowl, whisk together milk, eggs, and melted butter.Fold the wet ingredients into the dry ones until just combined. Gently stir in the blueberries.Set the Blackstone Griddle to 375°F and brush with a little butter.Pour 1/4 cup portions of the batter onto the griddle, spacing them apart.Cook until the edges set and bubbles form on top, about 2 minutes. Flip carefully and cook until browned on the other side, another 1-2 minutes.Serve the pancakes with lemon wedges and a drizzle of honey or maple syrup.

Nutritional values: Approx. 325 calories | 9g protein | 10g fats | 53g carbohydrates

3.2 Eggs: Over Easy to Scrambled

Recipe 1: Classic Over Easy Eggs

Preparation time = 5 minutes

Ingredients = 2 large eggs | Salt to taste | Pepper to taste | 1 tablespoon olive oil

Servings = Serves 1

Mode of cooking: Griddling

Procedure: Preheat your Blackstone Griddle over medium heat and brush it with olive oil.Crack the eggs onto the griddle, ensuring they don't touch. Season with salt and pepper.Cook for about 1-2 minutes until the whites are set but the yolks are still runny.Carefully flip each egg using a spatula and cook for another 30 seconds for a soft yolk or 1 minute for a firmer yolk.Serve immediately, ideal for breakfast alongside toast and bacon.

Nutritional values: 150 calories | 12g protein | 10g fats | 0g carbohydrates

---

Recipe 2: Griddled Scrambled Eggs

Preparation time = 5 minutes

Ingredients = 4 large eggs | 1/4 cup milk | Salt to taste | Pepper to taste | 2 tablespoons unsalted butter

Servings = Serves 2

Mode of cooking: Griddling

Procedure: In a bowl, whisk together the eggs, milk, salt, and pepper until well combined.Preheat the Blackstone Griddle to medium-low heat and melt the butter on its surface.Pour the egg mixture onto the griddle. Let it sit without stirring for about 20 seconds, then gently fold the eggs from the edges to the center with a spatula.Continue cooking, occasionally folding, until the eggs are softly set and slightly runny in places (about 2-3 minutes).Serve the scrambled eggs fluffy and light,

optionally topping with chopped herbs or shredded cheese.

Nutritional values: 215 calories | 14g protein | 16g fats | 2g carbohydrates

---

Recipe 3: Cheesy Griddle Omelette

Preparation time = 10 minutes

Ingredients = 3 large eggs | 1/4 cup shredded cheddar cheese | 1/4 cup diced bell peppers | 1/4 cup diced onions | Salt to taste | Pepper to taste | 1 tablespoon olive oil

Servings = Serves 1

Mode of cooking: Griddling

Procedure: Beat the eggs in a bowl. Stir in the cheese, bell peppers, onions, salt, and pepper.Heat the Blackstone Griddle to medium heat and drizzle with olive oil.Pour the egg mixture onto the griddle, forming an even circle. Cook without stirring for about 2 minutes until the edges start to lift from the griddle.Carefully flip the omelette and cook for an additional 1-2 minutes until the cheese is melted and the eggs are set.Fold the omelette in half on the griddle, then serve hot, possibly with a side of grilled tomatoes.

Nutritional values: 320 calories | 21g protein | 24g fats | 6g carbohydrates

---

Recipe 4: Sunny-Side Up Eggs with Spinach

Preparation time = 6 minutes

Ingredients = 2 large eggs | 1 cup fresh spinach | Salt to taste | Pepper to taste | 1 tablespoon olive oil | 1 teaspoon garlic, minced

Servings = Serves 1

Mode of cooking: Griddling

Procedure: Preheat your Blackstone Griddle over medium heat and add the olive oil.Add the minced garlic and sauté for about 30 seconds, then add the spinach and cook until just wilted, about 1 minute. Season with salt and pepper.Push the spinach to one side of the griddle. Crack the eggs into the cleared area, taking care not to break the yolks.Cook the eggs until the whites are completely set but the yolks are still runny, about 2-3 minutes. Season with salt and pepper.Carefully remove the eggs and spinach from the griddle and serve immediately, enjoying a healthy and flavorful breakfast.

Nutritional values: 220 calories | 13g protein | 17g fats | 3g carbohydrates

---

3.3 Sizzling Breakfast Meats

Recipe 1: Griddle-Seared Thick Cut Bacon.

Preparation time = 15 minutes

Ingredients = 1lb thick-cut bacon | 1 tsp black pepper | 1 tbsp maple syrup

Servings = Serves 4

Mode of cooking: Griddle

Procedure: Preheat your Blackstone griddle to medium-high heat.Lay the bacon strips flat on the griddle, ensuring they do not overlap.Cook until the bacon starts to crisp around the edges, then flip.Season with black pepper and drizzle maple syrup on top.Continue cooking until the bacon reaches the desired level of crispiness.Remove from the griddle and place on a paper towel to drain excess oil.

Nutritional values: 250 calories | 19g protein | 20g fats | 0g carbohydrates

Recipe 2: Spicy Griddle Sausage Patties.

Preparation time = 20 minutes

Ingredients = 1lb ground sausage | 1 tsp red pepper flakes | 1/2 tsp garlic powder | 1/2 tsp onion powder | Salt to taste

Servings = Serves 4

Mode of cooking: Griddle

Procedure: In a bowl, mix the ground sausage with red pepper flakes, garlic powder, onion powder, and salt. Place patties onto the preheated griddle set to medium heat.Cook for 4-5

minutes on each side or until golden brown and fully cooked through. Remove the patties from the griddle and allow them to rest for a moment before serving.

Nutritional values: 340 calories | 16g protein | 30g fats | 2g carbohydrates

Recipe 3: Honey-Glazed Griddle Ham.

Preparation time = 10 minutes

Ingredients = 4 slices of ham (about 1/2" thick) | 1/4 cup honey | 1 tsp mustard | 1 tsp brown sugar | Pinch of ground cloves

Servings = Serves 4

Mode of cooking: Griddle

Procedure: Preheat the griddle over medium heat.In a small bowl, mix honey, mustard, brown sugar, and ground cloves to create a glaze.Place the ham slices on the griddle and brush the glaze over the top.Cook for about 3 minutes on each side, brushing with more glaze if desired.Once the ham is caramelized transfer it to a plate to serve.

Nutritional values: 210 calories | 14g protein | 5g fats | 22g carbohydrates

Recipe 4: Griddle Breakfast Steak Strips.

Preparation time = 25 minutes

Ingredients = 1 lb flank steak | 1 tsp smoked paprika | Salt and pepper to taste | 1 tbsp olive oil

Servings = Serves 4

Mode of cooking: Griddle

Procedure: Slice the flank steak into thin strips and season with smoked paprika, salt, and pepper.
Preheat the griddle to high heat and brush it with olive oil.
Place the steak strips onto the griddle and cook for about 2-3 minutes on each side or until they reach the desired doneness.Remove the steak strips from the griddle and let them rest for a few minutes before serving.

Nutritional values: 220 calories | 26g protein | 10g fats | 0g carbohydrates

Chapter 4:

Lunch Favorites

4.1: Burgers: From Classic to Gourmet

Recipe 1: Classic Griddle Cheeseburger.

Preparation time = 20 minutes

Ingredients = 1lb ground beef (80/20) | 4 slices cheddar cheese | 4 hamburger buns | Salt and pepper to taste | Lettuce | Tomato slices | Red onion slices

Servings = Serves 4

Mode of cooking: Griddle

Procedure: Preheat your Blackstone griddle over medium-high heat.

Divide the ground beef into 4 equal parts and form them into patties. Season both sides with salt and pepper.

Place the patties on the griddle, cooking for about 4-5 minutes on each side for medium doneness.

A minute before the burgers are done, place a slice of cheddar cheese on each patty to melt.

Toast the buns on the griddle for a minute or until slightly crispy.

Assemble the burgers by placing lettuce, tomato, and onion on the bottom bun, then the cheese-topped patty, and cover with the top bun.

Nutritional values: 550 calories | 32g protein | 40g fats | 22g carbohydrates

---

Recipe 2: Smoky Bacon Avocado Burger.

Preparation time = 30 minutes

Ingredients = 1lb ground beef (80/20) | 8 slices smoked bacon | 2 ripe avocados | 1 tbsp lime juice | 4 burger buns | Salt and pepper to taste | Lettuce | Tomato slices

Servings = Serves 4

Mode of cooking: Griddle

Procedure: Cook the bacon on the preheated griddle until crisp, then set aside on paper towels to drain.
Mash the avocados in a bowl, mix with lime juice, and season with salt and pepper.Form the ground beef into 4 patties and season with salt and pepper. Cook on the griddle for 4-5 minutes on each side.Toast the buns lightly on the griddle.Assemble the burgers with a base of lettuce and tomato on the buns, add the beef patties, top with bacon, and a generous scoop of avocado mash.

Nutritional values: 690 calories | 35g protein | 50g fats | 31g carbohydrates

---

Recipe 3: Blue Cheese and Mushroom Burger.

Preparation time = 25 minutes

Ingredients = 1lb ground beef (80/20) | 4 oz blue cheese crumbles | 1 cup sliced mushrooms | 1 tbsp Worcestershire sauce | 4 burger buns | Salt and pepper | Olive oil | Arugula

Servings = Serves 4

Mode of cooking: Griddle

Procedure: Preheat the griddle to medium-high and sauté the mushrooms with a little olive oil until soft. Set aside. Mix the ground beef with Worcestershire sauce, salt, and pepper, then form into 4 patties.Cook the patties on the griddle for about 5 minutes on each side.In the last minute of cooking, top each patty with blue cheese crumbles and cover to melt.Toast the buns on the griddle, then assemble the burgers with a layer of arugula on the buns, followed by the cheese-melted patties and sautéed mushrooms.

Nutritional values: 600 calories | 38g protein | 42g fats | 22g carbohydrates

---

Recipe 4: Spicy Jalapeño and Cheddar Stuffed Burger.

Preparation time = 30 minutes

Ingredients = 1lb ground beef (80/20) | 1 jalapeño, finely diced | 4 oz cheddar cheese, diced | 4 burger buns | Salt and pepper | Lettuce | Tomato slices

Servings = Serves 4

Mode of cooking: Griddle

Procedure: In a bowl, mix the ground beef with diced jalapeños, salt, and pepper.
Divide the mix into 8 thin patties. Place diced cheddar on 4 patties, then cover each with another patty, sealing the edges.
Preheat the griddle to medium-high and cook the stuffed patties for about 6-7 minutes per side.

Toast the buns on the griddle.
Assemble the burgers by placing lettuce and tomato on the bottom bun, then the jalapeño-cheddar stuffed patty, topped with the other half of the bun.

Nutritional values: 650 calories | 40g protein | 47g fats | 23g carbohydrates

4.2 Sandwich Melts and Wraps

Recipe 1: Griddled Chicken Pesto Melt.

Preparation time = 25 minutes

Ingredients = 2 chicken breasts, grilled and sliced | 4 slices of sourdough bread | 1/4 cup pesto sauce | 8 slices mozzarella cheese | 1 tomato, sliced | Salt and pepper | Olive oil

Servings = Serves 4

Mode of cooking: Griddle

Procedure: Preheat your Blackstone griddle to medium heat and brush lightly with olive oil.
Spread pesto sauce on one side of each bread slice.
Layer mozzarella cheese, sliced chicken breast, tomato slices, and another layer of mozzarella on top of the pesto-spread side of the bread.
Top with another slice of bread, pesto side facing inwards.
Cook the sandwich on the griddle, pressing down slightly, for about 3-4 minutes on each side or until the bread is golden and the cheese has melted.

Cut the sandwiches in half and serve hot.

Nutritional values: 640 calories | 45g protein | 30g fats | 45g carbohydrates

---

Recipe 2: Spicy Griddle Steak Wrap.

Preparation time = 30 minutes

Ingredients = 1 lb flank steak | 4 large flour tortillas | 1/2 cup chipotle sauce | 2 cups lettuce, shredded | 1 avocado, sliced | 1/2 red onion, thinly sliced | Salt and pepper | Lime wedges

Servings = Serves 4

Mode of cooking: Griddle

Procedure: Season the flank steak with salt and pepper and let it sit at room temperature for about 15 minutes. Preheat your Blackstone griddle to high heat. Cook the steak for about 5-6 minutes on each side or to your desired doneness. Let it rest for 5 minutes, then slice thinly against the grain.
Warm the flour tortillas on the griddle for about 30 seconds on each side. Assemble the wraps by spreading chipotle sauce on each tortilla, then adding lettuce, avocado, red onion, and steak slices. Squeeze lime juice over the filling before rolling up the tortillas. Serve immediately with extra lime wedges.

Nutritional values: 580 calories | 38g protein | 28g fats | 46g carbohydrates

---

Recipe 3: Griddle Turkey and Cranberry Panini.

Preparation time = 20 minutes

Ingredients = 8 slices of ciabatta bread | 1 lb sliced turkey breast | 1/2 cup cranberry sauce | 8 slices Swiss cheese | 2 tbsp butter, softened | 1/4 cup arugula | Salt and pepper

Servings = Serves 4

Mode of cooking: Griddle

Procedure: Spread butter on one side of each bread slice.
On the unbuttered side of four bread slices, layer Swiss cheese, sliced turkey, cranberry sauce, and arugula. Season with salt and pepper. Top with the remaining bread slices, buttered side up. Preheat your Blackstone griddle to medium heat. Place the sandwiches on the griddle and press down softly with a spatula or a heavy pan.
Cook for about 4-5 minutes on each side, until the bread is toasted and the cheese has melted.
Cut the paninis in half and serve warm.

Nutritional values: 650 calories | 42g protein | 25g fats | 65g carbohydrates

---

Recipe 4: Veggie Hummus Griddle Wrap.

Preparation time = 20 minutes

Ingredients = 4 large whole wheat tortillas | 1 cup hummus | 1 cucumber, sliced thin | 1 bell pepper, sliced thin | 1/2 red onion, sliced thin | 2 carrots, shredded | 2 cups spinach leaves | Salt and pepper

Servings = Serves 4

Mode of cooking: None required for the wrap (But griddle for warming tortillas)

Procedure: Warm the tortillas on the preheated Blackstone griddle for about 30 seconds on each side.
Spread a quarter cup of hummus on each tortilla.
Distribute cucumber, bell pepper, red onion, carrots, and spinach evenly among the tortillas. Season with a bit of salt and pepper.
Carefully roll up the tortillas to enclose the filling.
Serve the wraps immediately, or wrap them in foil to keep them fresh if serving later.

Nutritional values: 350 calories | 12g protein | 9g fats | 58g carbohydrates

4.3 Healthy Grilled Salads

Recipe 1: Grilled Romaine with Lemon-Parmesan Dressing.

Preparation time = 15 minutes

Ingredients = 2 romaine lettuce hearts, halved lengthwise | 2 tbsp olive oil | Juice of 1 lemon | 1/4 cup grated Parmesan cheese | 1 tsp Dijon mustard | Salt and pepper | 1/4 cup whole wheat croutons

Servings = Serves 4

Mode of cooking: Griddle

Procedure: Preheat your Blackstone griddle to medium-high heat.
Brush the cut sides of the romaine lettuce with olive oil and season with salt and pepper.
Place the romaine cut side down on the griddle and grill until charred, about 2 to 3 minutes.
For the dressing, whisk together lemon juice, Dijon mustard, grated Parmesan cheese, salt, and pepper in a small bowl.
Drizzle the dressing over the grilled romaine and top with whole wheat croutons.

Nutritional values: 150 calories | 5g protein | 11g fats | 9g carbohydrates

Recipe 2: Griddled Mediterranean Vegetable Salad.

Preparation time = 20 minutes

Ingredients = 1 zucchini, sliced lengthwise | 1 yellow squash, sliced lengthwise | 1 red bell pepper, sliced | 1 eggplant, sliced | 2 tbsp balsamic vinegar | 3 tbsp olive oil | 1 tsp dried oregano | 1/2 cup feta cheese, crumbled | 1/4 cup olives, sliced | Salt and pepper

Servings = Serves 4

Mode of cooking: Griddle

Procedure: Preheat the Blackstone griddle to medium heat and coat with a thin layer of olive oil.

Season the zucchini, yellow squash, red bell pepper, and eggplant with salt, pepper, and dried oregano.
Grill the vegetables in batches, turning occasionally, until they are tender and have char marks, about 4 to 5 minutes per side.
Whisk together balsamic vinegar and olive oil in a large bowl.
Cut the grilled vegetables into bite-sized pieces and toss with the balsamic dressing. Gently mix in the feta cheese and olives.

Nutritional values: 220 calories | 5g protein | 18g fats | 12g carbohydrates

Recipe 3: Charred Corn and Avocado Salad.

Preparation time = 15 minutes

Ingredients = 4 ears of corn, husks removed | 1 avocado, diced | 1/2 red onion, finely chopped | 1 cup cherry tomatoes, halved | 1/4 cup cilantro, chopped | Juice of 1 lime | Salt and pepper | 1 tbsp olive oil
Servings = Serves 4
Mode of cooking: Griddle

Procedure: Preheat the Blackstone griddle to high heat.

Brush the corn with olive oil and season with salt and pepper.

Grill the corn, turning occasionally until charred on all sides, about 10 minutes.

Once cooled, cut the kernels off the cobs and transfer to a salad bowl.

Add the diced avocado, cherry tomatoes, red onion, and cilantro to the bowl.

Pour lime juice over the salad, season with salt and pepper, and toss gently to combine.

Nutritional values: 210 calories | 4g protein | 14g fats | 24g carbohydrates

Mode of cooking: Griddle

Procedure: Preheat the Blackstone griddle over medium heat.

Brush the pear slices with olive oil and grill until they have prominent grill marks, about 2 minutes on each side.

Arrange arugula on a serving platter and top with the grilled pear slices, toasted walnuts, and crumbled blue cheese.

Drizzle with balsamic glaze and season with salt and pepper to taste.

Nutritional values: 180 calories | 4g protein | 11g fats | 18g carbohydrates

Recipe 4: Grilled Pear and Arugula Salad.

Preparation time = 15 minutes

Ingredients = 2 ripe pears, cored and sliced | 4 cups arugula | 1/4 cup walnuts, toasted | 1/4 cup crumbled blue cheese | 2 tbsp balsamic glaze | Salt and pepper | 1 tbsp olive oil

Servings = Serves 4

Chapter 5:

Dinner Spectaculars

5.1: Searing Steaks to Perfection

Recipe 1: Classic Ribeye Steak.

Preparation time = 25 minutes

Ingredients = 2 ribeye steaks, 1-inch thick | 2 tbsp olive oil | 2 tsp coarse salt | 1 tsp freshly ground black pepper | 2 cloves garlic, minced | 1 tbsp butter

Servings = Serves 2

Mode of cooking: Griddle

Procedure: Bring steaks to room temperature, about 20 minutes before cooking.

Preheat the Blackstone griddle to high heat, around 400°F.Rub each steak with olive oil, then season both sides generously with salt, pepper, and garlic.Place steaks on the griddle, and cook for 4-5 minutes on each side for medium-rare, or longer for desired doneness.Towards the last minute of cooking, place a tablespoon of butter on top of each steak to melt.Remove steaks from the griddle, tent loosely with foil, and let rest for 5 minutes before serving to ensure juicy meat.

Nutritional values: 560 calories | 46g protein | 40g fats | 0g carbohydrates

Recipe 2: Herb-Crusted Flank Steak.

Preparation time = 30 minutes (plus marinating time)

Ingredients = 1 flank steak (about 1.5 pounds) | 1/4 cup olive oil | 3 cloves garlic, minced | 2 tbsp fresh rosemary, chopped | 2 tbsp fresh thyme, chopped | Salt and pepper

Servings = Serves 4

Mode of cooking: Griddle

Procedure: In a small bowl, mix olive oil, garlic, rosemary, thyme, salt, and pepper.Rub the herb mixture all over the flank steak and let it marinate in the refrigerator for at least 2 hours, or overnight for best results.
Preheat the Blackstone griddle to high heat.Remove the steak from the marinade and place it on the griddle. Cook for 5-6 minutes on each side for medium-rare, or adjust according to preference.Rest the steak for at least 5 minutes before slicing against the grain and serving.

Nutritional values: 380 calories | 32g protein | 25g fats | 2g carbohydrates

---

Recipe 3: Spiced Skirt Steak with Chimichurri Sauce.

Preparation time = 20 minutes (plus marinating time)

Ingredients = 1 skirt steak (about 1 pound) | 2 tsp cumin | 2 tsp smoked paprika | Salt and pepper | For the Chimichurri: 1 cup fresh parsley, chopped | 1/4 cup olive oil | 2 tbsp red

wine vinegar | 2 garlic cloves, minced | 1 tsp red pepper flakes

Servings = Serves 4

Mode of cooking: Griddle

Procedure: Season the skirt steak with cumin, smoked paprika, salt, and pepper. Let it marinate for at least 30 minutes.To make the chimichurri, mix parsley, olive oil, red wine vinegar, garlic, and red pepper flakes in a bowl. Set aside.Preheat the Blackstone griddle to high heat.Grill the steak for about 3-4 minutes on each side for medium-rare. Slice the steak against the grain and serve with the chimichurri sauce on top.

Nutritional values: 420 calories | 35g protein | 28g fats | 5g carbohydrates

---

Recipe 4: Garlic Butter New York Strip.

Preparation time = 20 minutes

Ingredients = 2 New York strip steaks, 1-inch thick | 2 tbsp olive oil | Salt and pepper | 4 cloves garlic, minced | 3 tbsp butter | 1 tbsp fresh parsley, chopped

Servings = Serves 2

Mode of cooking: Griddle

Procedure: Season the New York strip steaks with salt and pepper.
Preheat the Blackstone griddle over high heat.
Rub each steak with olive oil and place on the griddle. Cook for 4-5 minutes on each side for medium-rare.

In the last 2 minutes of cooking, add minced garlic and butter to the pan, allowing the butter to melt and garlic to soften. Spoon the garlic butter over the steaks continuously.
Remove the steaks, garnish with fresh parsley, and let rest for 5 minutes before serving.

Nutritional values: 580 calories | 47g protein | 42g fats | 2g carbohydrates

5.2 Griddling Chicken Dishes

Recipe 1: Griddle Lemon Herb Chicken.

Preparation time = 30 minutes

Ingredients = 4 chicken breasts | Juice of 1 lemon | 2 tbsp olive oil | 1 tbsp fresh rosemary, chopped | 1 tbsp fresh thyme, chopped | Salt and pepper

Servings = Serves 4

Mode of cooking: Griddle

Procedure: In a mixing bowl, combine lemon juice, olive oil, rosemary, thyme, salt, and pepper.Marinate the chicken breasts in the mixture for at least 20 minutes in the refrigerator.Preheat your Blackstone griddle to medium-high heat.Place the marinated chicken breasts on the griddle, cook for 6-7 minutes on each side or until the internal temperature reaches 165°F.Remove from the griddle and let rest for 5 minutes before serving.

Nutritional values: 220 calories | 26g protein | 12g fats | 1g carbohydrates

Recipe 2: Griddle BBQ Chicken Thighs.

Preparation time = 25 minutes

Ingredients = 8 chicken thighs, skin-on | 1 cup BBQ sauce | 2 tbsp olive oil | Salt and pepper | 1 tsp smoked paprika

Servings = Serves 4

Mode of cooking: Griddle

Procedure: Preheat the Blackstone griddle over medium heat.Season chicken thighs with salt, pepper, and smoked paprika.Brush the griddle with olive oil and place the chicken thighs skin-side down. Cook for about 10 minutes on each side.During the last 5 minutes of cooking, brush the BBQ sauce over the chicken thighs, flipping occasionally, until well coated and caramelized.Ensure chicken is fully cooked, with an internal temperature of 165°F before serving.

Nutritional values: 310 calories | 25g protein | 20g fats | 15g carbohydrates

Recipe 3: Griddle Chicken Fajitas.

Preparation time = 20 minutes (plus marinating time)

Ingredients = 3 chicken breasts, thinly sliced | 1 red bell pepper, sliced | 1 green bell pepper, sliced | 1 medium onion, sliced | 2 tbsp fajita seasoning | 2 tbsp olive oil | Juice of 1 lime

Servings = Serves 4

Mode of cooking: Griddle

Procedure: Marinate the sliced chicken with olive oil, lime juice, and fajita seasoning for at least 30 minutes. Preheat your Blackstone griddle to medium-high heat.
Cook the marinated chicken slices for 5-6 minutes, or until fully cooked, then remove from the griddle.
Add the sliced bell peppers and onion to the griddle, cooking until they are tender and slightly charred, about 7-8 minutes.
Return the chicken to the griddle, mix with the vegetables, and cook for an additional 2-3 minutes.
Serve with warm tortillas and your preferred fajita toppings.

Nutritional values: 260 calories | 28g protein | 9g fats | 16g carbohydrates

---

Recipe 4: Garlic Parmesan Griddle Chicken Wings.

Preparation time = 35 minutes

Ingredients = 2 lbs chicken wings | 4 cloves garlic, minced | 1/4 cup butter | 1/2 cup grated Parmesan cheese | Salt and pepper | 1 tsp parsley, chopped

Servings = Serves 4

Mode of cooking: Griddle

Procedure: Preheat your Blackstone griddle to medium heat.
Season the chicken wings with salt and pepper.
Cook the wings on the griddle, turning occasionally, until they are golden brown and the internal temperature reaches 165°F, about 20-25 minutes.
In a skillet over the griddle, melt butter and sauté garlic until fragrant.
Toss the cooked wings in the garlic butter, then sprinkle with grated Parmesan and parsley.
Serve immediately.

Nutritional values: 450 calories | 32g protein | 34g fats | 1g carbohydrates

---

5.3 Delicate Seafood Dishes

Recipe 1: Griddled Garlic Shrimp Skewers.

Preparation time = 20 minutes

Ingredients = 2 lbs large shrimp, peeled and deveined | 4 cloves garlic, minced | 2 tbsp olive oil | 1 tsp smoked paprika | Salt and pepper | 1 lemon,

Servings = Serves 4

Mode of cooking: Griddle

Procedure: Preheat the Blackstone griddle to medium-high heat.In a bowl, mix together shrimp, olive oil, garlic, smoked paprika, salt, and pepper until shrimp are evenly coated.
Thread the shrimp onto skewers.Place the skewers on the griddle, cooking each side for 2-3 minutes or until shrimp turn

pink and opaque.Serve the skewers with fresh lemon wedges on the side.

Nutritional values: 225 calories | 24g protein | 12g fats | 3g carbohydrates

Recipe 2: Griddled Lime Cilantro Scallops.

Preparation time = 15 minutes

Ingredients = 1 lb scallops | Juice of 2 limes | 1/4 cup fresh cilantro, chopped | 2 tbsp olive oil | Salt and pepper

Servings = Serves 4

Mode of cooking: Griddle

Procedure: Marinate scallops with lime juice, cilantro, olive oil, salt, and pepper for 10 minutes.
Heat the Blackstone griddle over medium-high heat.
Place the marinated scallops on the griddle, and cook for 2-3 minutes on each side, or until they have a nice sear and are opaque throughout.
Serve hot, garnished with additional fresh cilantro if desired.

Nutritional values: 150 calories | 14g protein | 9g fats | 4g carbohydrates

Recipe 3: Griddle-Smoked Salmon with Dill Sauce.

Preparation time = 25 minutes

Ingredients = 4 salmon fillets | 2 tbsp olive oil | Salt and pepper | 1/2 cup sour cream | 2 tbsp fresh dill, chopped | 1 tbsp lemon juice | 1 tsp garlic powder

Servings = Serves 4

Mode of cooking: Griddle

Procedure: Preheat the Blackstone griddle to medium heat.Season salmon fillets with salt and pepper, then brush each with olive oil.
Place salmon on the griddle, skin side down, and cook for 5-6 minutes or until the skin is crispy. Flip and cook for another 4-5 minutes on the other side. While salmon cooks, mix sour cream, dill, lemon juice, and garlic powder in a bowl for the dill sauce.Serve the salmon with dill sauce drizzled on top.

Nutritional values: 320 calories | 23g protein | 23g fats | 2g carbohydrates

Recipe 4: Chili-Lime Griddled Cod.

Preparation time = 20 minutes

Ingredients = 4 cod fillets | 1 tbsp chili powder | Zest and juice of 1 lime | 2 tbsp olive oil | Salt and pepper | 1 tbsp honey

Servings = Serves 4

Mode of cooking: Griddle

Procedure: In a small bowl, make a marinade by mixing the chili powder, lime zest and juice, olive oil, salt, pepper, and honey.
Coat the cod fillets evenly with the marinade and let them sit for 10 minutes.
Preheat the Blackstone griddle to medium-high heat.
Cook the cod fillets for about 4 minutes on each side or until they flake easily with a fork.
Serve hot, with extra lime wedges on the side if desired.

Nutritional values: 200 calories | 21g protein | 9g fats | 5g carbohydrates

Chapter 6:

Vegetarian and Vegan Options

6.1 Griddling Fresh Vegetables

Recipe 1: Griddled Balsamic Brussels Sprouts.

Preparation time = 25 minutes

Ingredients = 1 lb Brussels sprouts, halved | 2 tbsp olive oil | 3 tbsp balsamic vinegar | Salt and pepper | 1 tsp garlic powder

Servings = Serves 4

Mode of cooking: Griddle

Procedure: Preheat Blackstone griddle to medium-high heat.In a bowl, toss the Brussels sprouts with olive oil, balsamic vinegar, salt, pepper, and garlic powder until well coated.Place the Brussels sprouts cut side down on the griddle. Cook for about 10-12 minutes, turning occasionally, until they are charred and tender.

Serve hot, optionally drizzling with more balsamic vinegar if desired.

Nutritional values: 120 calories | 4g protein | 7g fats | 10g carbohydrates

Recipe 2: Griddle-Roasted Herb Potatoes.

Preparation time = 30 minutes

Ingredients = 2 lbs baby potatoes, halved | 3 tbsp olive oil | 1 tbsp rosemary, finely chopped | 1 tbsp thyme, finely chopped | Salt and pepper

Servings = Serves 4

Mode of cooking: Griddle

Procedure: Preheat the Blackstone griddle to medium heat.In a large bowl, mix the potatoes with olive oil, rosemary, thyme, salt, and pepper until evenly coated.Place the potatoes cut side down on the griddle and cover with a metal bowl or aluminum foil to trap in heat and moisture.Cook for about 20 minutes, stirring occasionally, until the potatoes are golden and tender.Serve immediately, garnished with more fresh herbs if desired.

Nutritional values: 200 calories | 4g protein | 10g fats | 28g carbohydrates

Recipe 3: Smoky Griddled Asparagus with Lemon.

Preparation time = 15 minutes

Ingredients = 1 lb asparagus, trimmed | 2 tbsp olive oil | Salt and smoked paprika | 1 lemon, cut into wedges

Servings = Serves 4

Mode of cooking: Griddle

Procedure: Preheat the Blackstone griddle to medium-high heat.
In a large bowl, toss the asparagus with olive oil, salt, and a generous sprinkle of smoked paprika.
Grill the asparagus on the griddle for about 5-7 minutes, turning frequently, until tender and charred.
Serve the asparagus with lemon wedges for squeezing over the top.

Nutritional values: 80 calories | 2.5g protein | 7g fats | 4g carbohydrates

Recipe 4: Caramelized Griddle Sweet Potatoes.

Preparation time = 35 minutes

Ingredients = 2 large sweet potatoes, thinly sliced | 2 tbsp butter, melted | 2 tbsp brown sugar | 1 tsp cinnamon | Salt

Servings = Serves 4

Mode of cooking: Griddle

Procedure: Preheat the Blackstone griddle to medium heat.
In a large bowl, combine the sweet potato slices, melted butter, brown

sugar, cinnamon, and a pinch of salt. Toss to coat evenly.

Arrange the sweet potato slices in a single layer on the griddle. Cook for about 15-20 minutes, turning occasionally, until they are tender and caramelized.

Serve warm as a delicious side dish.

Nutritional values: 220 calories | 2g protein | 6g fats | 42g carbohydrates

---

6.2 Innovative Tofu and Tempeh Recipes

Recipe 1: Griddled Tofu Steak with Chimichurri.

Preparation time = 30 minutes

Ingredients = 1 lb firm tofu, pressed and sliced into 1/2-inch steaks | 2 tbsp soy sauce | 1 tbsp olive oil | For Chimichurri: 1/2 cup fresh parsley | 1/4 cup olive oil | 2 tbsp red wine vinegar | 2 garlic cloves, minced | 1 tsp red pepper flakes | Salt and pepper

Servings = Serves 4

Mode of cooking: Griddle

Procedure:Marinate tofu steaks in soy sauce for 15 minutes.Preheat Blackstone griddle to medium-high. Brush griddle with olive oil.Grill tofu steaks for about 3-4 minutes per side, or until golden brown and crispy.For the chimichurri, combine parsley, olive oil, vinegar, garlic, red pepper flakes, salt, and pepper in a blender. Pulse until smooth. Serve tofu steaks drizzled with the chimichurri sauce.

Nutritional values: 225 calories | 12g protein | 17g fats | 7g carbohydrates

---

Recipe 2: Smoky Tempeh Breakfast Hash.

Preparation time = 45 minutes

Ingredients = 8 oz tempeh, crumbled | 2 tbsp soy sauce | 1 tsp smoked paprika | 2 tsp maple syrup | 1 sweet potato, diced

| 1 red bell pepper, diced | 1/2 onion, diced | 2 tbsp olive oil | Salt and pepper

Servings = Serves 4

Mode of cooking: Griddle

Procedure:Toss crumbled tempeh with soy sauce, smoked paprika, and maple syrup.Preheat Blackstone griddle to medium heat. Add olive oil.Sauté sweet potato, bell pepper, and onion on the griddle until softened, about 10 minutes.Add marinated tempeh and cook for another 15 minutes, stirring occasionally, until crispy and browned.Season with salt and pepper to taste. Serve the breakfast hash hot.

Nutritional values: 260 calories | 14g protein | 12g fats | 28g carbohydrates

---

Recipe 3: Griddled Tofu with Spicy Peanut Sauce.

Preparation time = 25 minutes

Ingredients = 1 lb firm tofu, pressed and sliced | For sauce: 1/4 cup peanut butter | 2 tbsp soy sauce | 1 tbsp lime juice | 1 tbsp honey | 1 garlic clove, minced | 1 tsp ginger, grated | 1-2 tsp sriracha or to taste | Water to thin | 1 tbsp sesame seeds for garnish

Servings = Serves 4

Mode of cooking: Griddle

Procedure: Preheat Blackstone griddle to medium-high. Lightly oil the surface. Cook tofu slices for 4-5 minutes on each side, until golden and crispy.For the peanut sauce, whisk together peanut butter, soy sauce, lime juice, honey, garlic, ginger, sriracha, and enough water to achieve desired consistency.Drizzle tofu with spicy peanut sauce and sprinkle sesame seeds on top before serving.

Nutritional values: 290 calories | 20g protein | 18g fats | 12g carbohydrates

---

Recipe 4: Zesty Lime Tempeh Tacos.

Preparation time = 30 minutes

Ingredients = 8 oz tempeh, sliced | Juice of 2 limes | 2 tbsp soy sauce | 1 tsp chili powder | 1 tsp cumin | 1 avocado, sliced | 8 small corn tortillas | 1/4 cup cilantro, chopped | 1 lime, cut into wedges | Salt and pepper

Servings = Serves 4

Mode of cooking: Griddle

Procedure: Marinate tempeh in lime juice, soy sauce, chili powder, cumin, salt, and pepper for 20 minutes. Preheat Blackstone griddle to medium-high. Cook tempeh for 3-4 minutes on each side, or until browned and heated through.

Warm corn tortillas on the griddle for about 30 seconds each side.

Assemble tacos with tempeh, avocado slices, and chopped cilantro. Serve with lime wedges on the side.

Nutritional values: 300 calories | 17g protein | 14g fats | 33g carbohydrates

---

6.3 Legumes and Grains on the Griddle

Recipe 1: Griddled Chickpea Patties.

Preparation time = 40 minutes

Ingredients = 1 can (15 oz) chickpeas, drained and rinsed | 1/2 onion, finely diced | 2 cloves garlic, minced | 1 tsp cumin | 1 tsp paprika | Salt and pepper | 2 tbsp olive oil | 1/4 cup fresh parsley, chopped

Servings = Serves 4

Mode of cooking: Griddle

Procedure: Mash chickpeas in a bowl until mostly smooth. Mix in onion, garlic, cumin, paprika, salt, pepper, and parsley.

Form the mixture into small patties, about 2 inches in diameter.

Preheat Blackstone griddle over medium heat and brush with olive oil.

Cook patties for 3-4 minutes on each side, or until they are golden brown and crispy.

Serve hot as an appetizer or a side dish.

Nutritional values: 220 calories | 8g protein | 10g fats | 28g carbohydrates

---

Recipe 2: Quinoa and Vegetable Stir-Fry.

Preparation time = 25 minutes

Ingredients = 1 cup quinoa, cooked | 1/4 cup soy sauce | 1 tbsp sesame oil | 1 cup broccoli florets | 1 red bell pepper, thinly sliced | 1/2 cup carrot, julienned | 1/2 onion, sliced | 2 cloves garlic, minced | 1 tsp ginger, grated

Servings = Serves 4

Mode of cooking: Griddle

Procedure: In a large bowl, toss the cooked quinoa with soy sauce and sesame oil.
Preheat your Blackstone griddle to medium-high heat.
Sauté broccoli, bell pepper, carrot, onion, garlic, and ginger on the griddle for about 5 minutes, or until vegetables are tender-crisp.
Add the quinoa mixture to the griddle and stir-fry everything together for another 5 minutes.
Serve hot, garnished with sesame seeds if desired.

Nutritional values: 260 calories | 9g protein | 7g fats | 42g carbohydrates

---

Recipe 3: Lentil Taco Filling.

Preparation time = 30 minutes

Ingredients = 1 cup brown lentils, cooked | 1 tbsp olive oil | 1 onion, finely chopped | 2 cloves garlic, minced | 1 tbsp chili powder | 1 tsp cumin | 1/2 tsp paprika | Salt and pepper | 1/4 cup tomato sauce

Servings = Serves 4

Mode of cooking: Griddle

Procedure: Preheat the Blackstone griddle over medium heat and add the olive oil.
Sauté the onion and garlic until soft and fragrant.
Add the cooked lentils, chili powder, cumin, paprika, salt, and pepper. Stir well to combine.
Mix in the tomato sauce and cook for another 5-10 minutes, until the mixture is heated through and flavors are blended.
Use the lentil mixture as a filling for tacos, topped with your favorite taco toppings.

Nutritional values: 210 calories | 12g protein | 4g fats | 34g carbohydrates

---

Recipe 4: Barley and Mushroom Pilaf.

Preparation time = 45 minutes

Ingredients = 1 cup pearled barley, rinsed | 2 tbsp olive oil | 1 lb mushrooms, sliced | 1 onion, diced | 2 cloves garlic, minced | 3 cups vegetable broth | 1/2 tsp thyme | Salt and pepper | 1/4 cup parsley, chopped

Servings = Serves 4

Mode of cooking: Griddle

Procedure:Preheat Blackstone griddle over medium heat. Add 1 tbsp olive oil and sauté mushrooms until golden brown. Remove and set aside.
In the same griddle, add the remaining olive oil and sauté onion and garlic until soft.
Add barley, stirring for about 2 minutes to lightly toast.Gradually pour in vegetable broth, stirring constantly. Add thyme, salt, and pepper.Cover with a griddle dome or aluminum foil and cook for 30 minutes, or until the barley is tender and the liquid is absorbed.Stir in the sautéed mushrooms and parsley before serving.

Nutritional values: 350 calories | 9g protein | 8g fats | 64g carbohydrates

---

Chapter 7:

Snacks and Appetizers

7.1: Finger Foods and Dipping Platters

Recipe 1: Griddled Mini Quesadillas.

Preparation time = 20 minutes

Ingredients = 8 small flour tortillas | 1 cup cheddar cheese, shredded | 1/2 cup cooked black beans | 1/2 cup corn kernels | 1 jalapeño, finely diced | 1/2 teaspoon ground cumin | Salt to taste | Olive oil for griddle

Servings = Serves 4

Mode of cooking: Griddle

Procedure: Heat Blackstone griddle to medium-high. Brush lightly with olive oil. On one half of each tortilla, sprinkle a portion of cheese, black beans, corn, jalapeño, cumin, and a pinch of salt. Fold the other half over the fillings to create a half-moon shape. Press down gently. Place quesadillas on the griddle and cook for about 2-3 minutes on each side or until the tortillas are golden brown and the cheese has melted. Cut into wedges and serve with your choice of salsa or sour cream.

Nutritional values: 280 calories | 12g protein | 14g fats | 30g carbohydrates

---

Recipe 2: Crispy Griddled Potato Skins.

Preparation time = 1 hour

Ingredients = 4 large russet potatoes | 1/4 cup olive oil | 1/2 cup bacon, cooked and crumbled | 1 cup cheddar cheese, shredded | 1/4 cup green onions, sliced | Salt and pepper to taste | Sour cream for serving

Servings = Serves 4

Mode of cooking: Griddle

Procedure: Preheat oven to 400°F (204°C). Bake potatoes for 45 minutes, or until fork-tender. Allow to cool. Cut the potatoes in half lengthwise, scoop out most of the flesh (leave about 1/4 inch), and cut each shell in half again to make quarters.Preheat Blackstone griddle to medium heat. Brush potato skins with olive oil, season with salt and pepper, and place on griddle.Grill skins for 2-3 minutes on each side until crispy.Sprinkle cheese and bacon into each skin. Close the griddle or cover with a dome to melt the cheese, about 2 minutes.Garnish with green onions and serve with a side of sour cream.

Nutritional values: 340 calories | 15g protein | 17g fats | 33g carbohydrates

---

Recipe 3: Griddled Chicken Satay Skewers.

Preparation time = 45 minutes (including marinating time)

Ingredients = 1 lb chicken breast, cut into strips | 1/4 cup coconut milk | 1 tablespoon curry powder | 1 tablespoon brown sugar | 1 garlic clove, minced | 1 teaspoon ginger, grated | 1 tablespoon soy sauce | Peanut sauce for dipping | Skewers

Servings = Serves 4

Mode of cooking: Griddle

Procedure: In a bowl, combine coconut milk, curry powder, brown sugar, garlic, ginger, and soy sauce. Add chicken strips and marinate for at least 30 minutes.Preheat Blackstone griddle to medium-high heat.Thread the marinated chicken strips onto skewers.Place skewers on the griddle and cook for 3-4 minutes per side or until fully cooked and nicely charred. Serve the chicken satay skewers with peanut sauce for dipping.

Nutritional values: 265 calories | 26g protein | 9g fats | 18g carbohydrates

---

Recipe 4: Griddled Halloumi Bites.

Preparation time = 15 minutes

Ingredients = 8 oz halloumi cheese, cut into bite-sized cubes | 1 tablespoon olive oil | 1 lemon, zested and juiced | 1 teaspoon dried oregano | Cherry tomatoes for garnish | Toothpicks

Servings = Serves 4

Mode of cooking: Griddle

Procedure: In a bowl, toss halloumi with olive oil, lemon zest, lemon juice, and oregano.

Preheat Blackstone griddle to medium heat.
Skewer halloumi cubes with toothpicks and place on the griddle.
Grill for 2-3 minutes on each side or until golden brown and crispy.
Serve immediately with cherry tomatoes and extra lemon wedges if desired.

Nutritional values: 300 calories | 19g protein | 22g fats | 5g carbohydrates

---

7.2 Stuffed Breads and Quesadillas

Recipe 1: Griddle-Baked Cheesy Garlic Bread.

Preparation time = 15 minutes

Ingredients = 1 loaf Italian bread | 1/2 cup unsalted butter, softened | 4 cloves garlic, minced | 1 tablespoon fresh parsley, chopped | 1 cup mozzarella cheese, shredded | 1/4 cup Parmesan cheese, grated | Salt and pepper to taste

Servings = Serves 8

Mode of cooking: Griddle

Procedure: Preheat Blackstone griddle to low heat and cover to create an oven-like environment.
Split the Italian bread in half lengthwise.
In a small bowl, mix the softened butter with garlic, parsley, salt, and pepper. Spread this mixture evenly on the cut sides of the bread.
Sprinkle both halves with mozzarella and Parmesan cheeses.
Place bread halves on the griddle, cut side up. Close the griddle top or cover with a dome. Cook for 7-10 minutes, or until the cheese is melted and bubbly.
Slice and serve warm.

Nutritional values: 310 calories | 11g protein | 18g fats | 27g carbohydrates

---

Recipe 2: Smoky BBQ Chicken Quesadilla.

Preparation time = 25 minutes

Ingredients = 2 chicken breasts, cooked and shredded | 1/2 cup BBQ sauce | 4 large flour tortillas | 1 cup cheddar cheese, shredded | 1 cup Gouda cheese, shredded | 1/2 red onion, thinly sliced | Cilantro for garnish | Olive oil for brushing

Servings = Serves 4

Mode of cooking: Griddle
Procedure: In a bowl, toss the shredded chicken with BBQ sauce until well coated.Heat the Blackstone griddle to medium-high heat and brush with olive oil.Lay out the flour tortillas on the griddle and evenly distribute the BBQ chicken, cheddar cheese, Gouda cheese, and red onion onto half of each tortilla. Fold the tortillas in half over the filling and press gently to seal.Cook for 3-4 minutes on each side, or until the tortilla is crispy and golden brown and the cheese is melted.Remove from the griddle, let cool for 1 minute, then cut into wedges. Garnish with cilantro and serve.

Nutritional values: 560 calories | 35g protein | 24g fats | 46g carbohydrates

Recipe 3: Griddle-Seared Stuffed Naan.

Preparation time = 30 minutes

Ingredients = 4 naan breads | 1 cup ricotta cheese | 1/2 cup sun-dried tomatoes, chopped | 1/4 cup Kalamata olives, pitted and chopped | 1 tablespoon fresh oregano, chopped | 2 cups spinach, wilted | Salt and pepper to taste | Olive oil for griddle

Servings = Serves 4

Mode of cooking: Griddle

Procedure: Preheat Blackstone griddle to medium heat.
In a bowl, combine ricotta, sun-dried tomatoes, olives, oregano, and wilted spinach. Season with salt and pepper. Spread the mixture over half of each naan bread. Fold the other half over to cover.Brush the griddle with olive oil and place the stuffed naans on it. Cook for about 3-4 minutes on each side until the naan is crispy and

golden-brown.Serve warm, cut into wedges or halves.

Nutritional values: 450 calories | 15g protein | 20g fats | 52g carbohydrates

---

Recipe 4: Sweet Apple-Cinnamon Stuffed French Toast.

Preparation time = 20 minutes

Ingredients = 1 French baguette | 1 cup cream cheese, softened | 2 apples, thinly sliced | 1/4 cup brown sugar | 1 teaspoon cinnamon | 4 eggs | 1/2 cup milk | 1/2 teaspoon vanilla extract | Maple syrup for serving | Butter for griddle

Servings = Serves 4

Mode of cooking: Griddle

Procedure:Cut the French baguette into 1-inch thick slices. Make a pocket in each slice by cutting horizontally without going all the way through. In a bowl, combine the cream cheese, brown sugar, and cinnamon. Spread this mixture inside the pockets of the bread slices, then add a few apple slices to each.In another bowl, whisk together eggs, milk, and vanilla extract. Dip the stuffed bread slices into the egg mixture, ensuring both sides are well-coated.Heat the Blackstone griddle to medium-low heat and add butter. Place the prepared bread slices on the griddle and cook for 4-5 minutes per side until golden brown and cooked through.Serve hot with maple syrup drizzled on top.

Nutritional values: 510 calories | 14g protein | 26g fats | 58g carbohydrates

---

7.3 Skewers and Kebabs

Recipe 1: Griddle-Grilled Veggie Skewers

Preparation time = 20 minutes

Ingredients = 2 zucchinis | 2 bell peppers (1 red, 1 yellow) | 1 red onion | 2 tablespoons olive oil | 1 teaspoon garlic powder | Salt and pepper to taste | 8 wooden skewers (soaked in water)

Servings = Serves 4

Mode of cooking: Griddle

Procedure:Preheat Blackstone griddle to medium-high heat.

Cut zucchinis, bell peppers, and red onion into bite-sized pieces.

Thread the vegetables onto the soaked skewers, alternating between zucchinis, bell peppers, and onions.

In a small bowl, mix the olive oil with garlic powder, salt, and pepper. Brush this mixture over the skewered veggies. Place skewers on the griddle and cook for 10-12 minutes, turning occasionally, until vegetables are tender and charred at the edges.

Nutritional values: 120 calories | 2g protein | 7g fats | 13g carbohydrates

Recipe 2: Honey-Glazed Chicken Skewers

Preparation time = 30 minutes

Ingredients = 1 lb chicken breast | 1/4 cup honey | 2 tablespoons soy sauce | 1 tablespoon olive oil | 1 garlic clove, minced | 1 teaspoon ginger, grated | Salt and pepper to taste | 8 wooden skewers (soaked in water)

Servings = Serves 4

Mode of cooking: Griddle

Procedure:Cut chicken breast into bite-sized pieces. In a bowl, combine honey, soy sauce, olive oil, garlic, ginger, salt, and pepper.Add chicken to the bowl and marinate for 15-20 minutes.Thread the marinated chicken onto the soaked skewers.Preheat Blackstone griddle to medium-high heat. Place skewers on the griddle and cook for about 5-7 minutes on each side, or until chicken is thoroughly cooked and glaze is caramelized.

Nutritional values: 220 calories | 25g protein | 6g fats | 18g carbohydrates

Recipe 3: Spicy Shrimp and Sausage Skewers

Preparation time = 25 minutes

Ingredients = 1 lb large shrimp, peeled and deveined | 1/2 lb spicy sausage, sliced | 2 tablespoons Cajun seasoning | 1 tablespoon olive oil | 8 wooden skewers

Servings = Serves 4

Mode of cooking: Griddle

Procedure:Preheat Blackstone griddle to medium-high heat.In a bowl, toss shrimp and sliced sausage with Cajun seasoning and olive oil.Thread shrimp and sausage slices onto the soaked skewers, alternating between them.Place skewers on the griddle and cook for 5-6 minutes on each side, until shrimp are pink and opaque and sausage is heated through.

Nutritional values: 310 calories | 23g protein | 20g fats | 5g carbohydrates

marinade, mix well, and let it marinate for 30 minutes.Cut red onion and bell pepper into bite-sized pieces.Thread marinated beef, onion, and pepper onto the soaked skewers.Preheat Blackstone griddle to medium-high heat. Cook skewers, turning occasionally, until beef is cooked to desired doneness.

Nutritional values: 330 calories | 25g protein | 15g fats | 18g carbohydrate

Recipe 4: Griddle-Seared Beef Kebabs

Preparation time = 40 minutes

Ingredients = 1 lb beef cubes (sirloin or tenderloin) | 1/4 cup soy sauce | 2 tablespoons brown sugar | 1 tablespoon sesame oil | 1 garlic clove, minced | 1 teaspoon black pepper | 1 red onion | 1 bell pepper | 8 wooden skewers

Servings = Serves 4

Mode of cooking: Griddle

Procedure:In a bowl, whisk together soy sauce, brown sugar, sesame oil, garlic, and black pepper to make a marinade.Add beef cubes to the

Chapter 8:

Desserts

8.1: Griddled Fruit Delicacies

Recipe 1: Griddled Pineapple with Cinnamon Honey Drizzle

Preparation time = 15 minutes

Ingredients = 1 pineapple, peeled and cored | 2 tablespoons honey | 1/2 teaspoon ground cinnamon | 1 tablespoon coconut oil

Servings = Serves 4

Mode of cooking: Griddle

Procedure:Cut the pineapple into rings or long slices, about 1/2 inch thick. Preheat the Blackstone griddle to medium heat and brush with coconut oil.Place pineapple slices on the griddle and cook for 2-3 minutes on each side or until they have nice grill marks.
In a small bowl, mix honey and ground cinnamon.
Drizzle the cinnamon honey over the warm grilled pineapple before serving.

Nutritional values: 100 calories | 0.5g protein | 0.5g fats | 25g Carbohydrates

Recipe 2: Griddle-Seared Peaches with Vanilla Ice Cream

Preparation time = 20 minutes

Ingredients = 4 peaches, halved and pitted | 2 tablespoons brown sugar | 1 teaspoon vanilla extract | 4 scoops vanilla ice cream | 1 tablespoon butter
Servings = Serves 4

Mode of cooking: Griddle

Procedure:Preheat Blackstone griddle over medium heat and melt the butter. Sprinkle the cut side of peaches with brown sugar and vanilla extract.
Place peaches, cut side down, on the griddle and cook for 4-5 minutes, or until they are caramelized and have grill marks.
Serve warm peach halves with a scoop of vanilla ice cream on top.

Nutritional values: 210 calories | 3g protein | 8g fats | 34g carbohydrates

---

Recipe 3: Caramelized Bananas with Rum Sauce

Preparation time = 15 minutes

Ingredients = 4 bananas, sliced in half lengthwise | 1/4 cup dark rum | 2

tablespoons brown sugar | 1 teaspoon cinnamon | 2 tablespoons butter

Servings = Serves 4

Mode of cooking: Griddle

Procedure:In a small saucepan, combine dark rum, brown sugar, and cinnamon. Cook over medium heat until sugar is dissolved, set aside.Preheat the Blackstone griddle to medium-high heat and melt the butter.Place bananas, cut side down, on the griddle, and cook for 2 minutes or until they start to caramelize. Flip the bananas and brush with the rum sauce. Cook for another minute.
Serve the caramelized bananas with extra rum sauce drizzled over the top.

Nutritional values: 180 calories | 1g protein | 3.5g fats | 36g carbohydrates

---

Recipe 4: Griddle-Baked Apples with Cinnamon Sugar

Preparation time = 25 minutes

Ingredients = 4 apples, cored and sliced | 2 tablespoons butter | 4 tablespoons brown sugar | 1 teaspoon ground cinnamon

Servings = Serves 4

Mode of cooking: Griddle

Procedure:Preheat the Blackstone griddle to medium heat and add the

butter.Mix the brown sugar and cinnamon in a small bowl.
Place the apple slices on the griddle and sprinkle with the cinnamon sugar mixture.Cook for about 5 minutes on each side, until the apples are soft and caramelized.Serve the griddle-baked apples warm, either as is or with a dollop of whipped cream or ice cream.

Nutritional values: 150 calories | 0.5g protein | 6g fats | 27g carbohydrates

---

8.2: Sweet Crepes and Grilled Donuts

<u>Recipe 1: Classic French Crepes with Chocolate Hazelnut Spread</u>

Preparation time = 30 minutes

Ingredients = 1 cup all-purpose flour | 2 eggs | 1 1/2 cups milk | 1 tablespoon sugar | 1 pinch salt | Butter for cooking | Chocolate hazelnut spread for filling

Servings = Serves 4

Mode of cooking: Griddle

Procedure: In a large mixing bowl, whisk together the flour, eggs, milk, sugar, and salt until smooth.Heat the Blackstone griddle over medium-low heat and lightly butter the surface.Pour or scoop the batter onto the griddle, using approximately 1/4 cup for each crepe. Tilt the griddle in a circular motion so that the batter coats the surface evenly.Cook for about 2 minutes, until the bottom is light brown. Loosen with a spatula, turn and cook the other side.Spread chocolate hazelnut spread over the crepe, fold, and serve warm.

Nutritional values: 290 calories | 8g protein | 14g fats | 34g carbohydrates

---

<u>Recipe 2: Griddled Donuts with Cinnamon Sugar</u>

Preparation time = 15 minutes (plus time for store-bought or pre-made dough to rise)

Ingredients = 1 can of refrigerated

biscuit dough | 1/2 cup sugar | 1 tablespoon ground cinnamon | 4 tablespoons butter, melted

Servings = Serves 8

Mode of cooking: Griddle

Procedure:Preheat the Blackstone griddle over medium heat.
Cut holes in the center of each biscuit dough to create donuts and donut holes. Place donuts and donut holes on the griddle, cooking for about 2 minutes on each side or until golden brown and cooked through.Mix sugar and cinnamon in a bowl. Brush each donut with melted butter, then toss with the cinnamon sugar mixture.

Nutritional values: 250 calories | 4g protein | 12g fats | 34g carbohydrates

---

Recipe 3: Chocolate Stuffed Crepes with Fresh Berries

Preparation time = 40 minutes

Ingredients = 1 cup all-purpose flour | 2 eggs | 1 1/2 cups milk | 2 tablespoons

cocoa powder | 1 tablespoon sugar | 1 pinch salt | Butter for cooking | Chocolate chips for filling | Fresh strawberries and raspberries for serving

Servings = Serves 4

Mode of cooking: Griddle

Procedure:In a large mixing bowl, whisk together flour, eggs, milk, cocoa powder, sugar, and salt until smooth. Heat the Blackstone griddle over medium-low heat and lightly butter the surface.Pour or scoop the batter onto the griddle, using approximately 1/4 cup for each crepe. Spread the batter to form thin crepes.Cook until the edges begin to slightly lift, about 2 minutes, then sprinkle chocolate chips over half the crepe.Fold the crepe in half over the chocolate chips, press down gently, and cook until chocolate is melted.
Serve with fresh berries on top.

Nutritional values: 320 calories | 9g protein | 14g fats | 42g carbohydrates

---

Recipe 4: Lemon Blueberry Crepes with Whipped Cream

Preparation time = 35 minutes

Ingredients = 1 cup all-purpose flour | 2 eggs | 1 1/2 cups milk | 1 tablespoon sugar | Lemon zest from 1 lemon | 1 cup fresh or frozen blueberries | Whipped cream for topping

Servings = Serves 4

Mode of cooking: Griddle

Procedure:In a large bowl, mix together the flour, eggs, milk, sugar, and lemon zest until the batter is smooth. Preheat the Blackstone griddle over medium-low heat and grease lightly with butter.Pour the batter onto the griddle, forming thin crepes, and sprinkle blueberries over each one while cooking. Cook each crepe for about 2 minutes on one side, then flip and cook for an additional minute on the other side.

Serve the crepes topped with whipped cream and additional blueberries if desired.

Nutritional values: 280 calories | 8g protein | 9g fats | 42g carbohydrates

---

8.3 S'mores and Campfire Classics

Recipe 1: Classic Griddle S'mores

Preparation time = 10 minutes

Ingredients = Graham crackers | Milk chocolate bars | Marshmallows

Servings = Serves 4

Mode of cooking: Griddle

Procedure:Preheat the Blackstone griddle to low heat.Break graham crackers in half and chocolate bars into sizes that will fit the crackers. Place marshmallows on the griddle and toast them, turning frequently until they are golden brown on all sides.Once marshmallows are toasted, place a chocolate piece on one graham cracker half, top with the hot marshmallow, then cover with the other graham cracker half, gently pressing down.

Serve immediately while the chocolate is still melting.

Nutritional values: 150 calories | 2g protein | 5g fats | 24g carbohydrates

---

Recipe 2: Campfire Apple Pie Packets

Preparation time = 25 minutes

Ingredients = Apples | Cinnamon sugar | Butter | Aluminum foil

Servings = Serves 4

Mode of cooking: Griddle

Procedure:Preheat the Blackstone griddle to medium heat.
Thinly slice apples and place them on a large square of aluminum foil.
Sprinkle apples with cinnamon sugar and dot with small pieces of butter.
Fold foil over the apples, sealing the edges to form a packet.
Place the packet on the griddle and cook for about 15-20 minutes, flipping halfway through.
Carefully open the packet (watch for steam), and serve warm.

Nutritional values: 210 calories | 1g protein | 11g fats | 28g carbohydrates

---

Recipe 3: Griddled Chocolate Banana Boats

Preparation time = 15 minutes

Ingredients = Bananas | Chocolate chips | Mini marshmallows | Aluminum foil

Servings = Serves 4

Mode of cooking: Griddle

Procedure:Preheat the Blackstone griddle to low heat.Make a lengthwise cut into each banana, ensuring not to cut through completely.Stuff chocolate chips and mini marshmallows into the slit.Wrap each banana completely in aluminum foil.Place wrapped bananas on the griddle and cook for about 5-10 minutes, until the chocolate and marshmallows have melted.Unwrap carefully and enjoy warm.

Nutritional values: 180 calories | 2g protein | 6g fats | 32g carbohydrates

---

Recipe 4: Peanut Butter Cup Griddle S'mores

Preparation time = 12 minutes

Ingredients = Graham crackers | Peanut butter cups | Marshmallows

Servings = Serves 4

Mode of cooking: Griddle

Procedure:Heat the Blackstone griddle to low heat.Place marshmallows on the griddle and toast until golden on all sides.Once marshmallows are toasted, place a peanut butter cup on one graham cracker half, top with the hot marshmallow, then cover with another graham cracker half.Serve immediately, pressing gently to melt the peanut butter cup with the marshmallow heat.

Nutritional values: 250 calories | 4g protein | 13g fats | 30g carbohydrates

Chapter 9:

Maintenance, Troubleshooting, and Safety Practices

9.1 Regular Cleaning Routines

Proper maintenance ensures that your griddle not only lasts longer but also consistently delivers the high-quality performance you've come to cherish for all your outdoor cooking. This chapter is dedicated to guiding you through the essential steps of maintaining your Blackstone griddle, specifically focusing on establishing regular cleaning routines that are both effective and manageable.

The Importance of Consistency

Cleaning might not be the most glamorous part of outdoor cooking, but its importance cannot be overstated. Without regular maintenance, your griddle can suffer from build-up that affects cooking performance, flavors, and can potentially be a health hazard. Establishing daily, weekly, and monthly cleaning routines is crucial in preventing these issues from arising, guaranteeing that every meal you cook is as delicious and safe as the first.

After Every Use: The Daily Routine

The cornerstone of griddle maintenance is the cleaning you do after each cooking session. While the griddle is still warm (but not scorching hot), use a metal scraper to remove food particles and cooking residue. This is crucial as it prevents the build-up of grime and keeps your cooking surface clean and non-stick. Once you've scraped down the surface, follow up with a few squirts of water (or a vinegar solution for a deeper clean) and scrub using a griddle brick or scouring pad. This method not only cleans but also helps in maintaining the seasoned surface of your griddle.

After the griddle has been scrubbed clean, rinse the surface with a cloth and clean water to remove any cleaning solution or loose debris. Dry the surface thoroughly with a cloth or paper towels. Finally, apply a thin layer of cooking oil, spreading it evenly over the surface. This acts as a protective coating, preventing rust and keeping the griddle seasoned.

The Weekly Deep Clean

Even with daily cleaning, your griddle can benefit from a deeper clean once a week, especially if used frequently. This involves a more detailed process to remove any tough stains or residues that daily cleaning might miss. Begin by heating your griddle to help loosen any residue. Use a griddle cleaning solution mixed with hot water and scrub the entire surface with a griddle brush or scouring pad. Pay special attention to corners and edges where grime tends to accumulate.

Once thoroughly scrubbed, rinse the surface with clean water, making sure no cleaning solution is left behind. Dry the surface entirely with towels, and, as with daily cleaning, finish by coating the surface with a thin layer of oil. This deep-cleaning process ensures that any stubborn residues are removed, keeping your griddle in prime condition.

Monthly Inspections and Maintenance

Beyond cleaning, a monthly check-up of your griddle can help nip potential issues in the bud. Inspect all components of your griddle, including the burners, igniter, and propane connections (for gas models). Look for any signs of wear, rust, or deterioration. Keeping the burners clean is essential for even heating; they can be cleaned with a metal brush to remove any debris that might be blocking the gas flow.

Additionally, re-season your griddle surface monthly to maintain its non-stick properties. This involves heating the griddle, applying a layer of cooking oil, and letting it burn off until the oil stops smoking, repeating the process a few times. This not only enhances the flavor of your food but also reinforces the griddle's resistance to rust and wear.

The Role of Storage

Proper storage plays a pivotal role in the longevity of your Blackstone griddle. Whenever your griddle is not in use, especially for extended periods, ensure it is stored in a dry, covered location. Use a griddle cover to protect it from the elements and prevent rust. Additionally, storing your griddle properly can save you time on cleaning and maintenance in the long run, as it minimizes exposure to moisture and outdoor debris.

9.2 Seasoning: When and How

The Art of Seasoning: A Primer

Seasoning isn't just a one-time task—it's an ongoing commitment to your griddle's performance and longevity. Think of seasoning as your griddle's best defense against rust and a proponent of that enviable black non-stick surface that makes cooking a breeze. But what is seasoning exactly? In the simplest terms, seasoning your griddle involves baking a high-smoke-point oil into the surface, creating a protective and naturally non-stick layer.

When to Season Your Griddle

Consistent seasoning is key to maintaining the optimum performance of your Blackstone griddle. Initially, seasoning occurs when you first bring your griddle home.

Regular re-seasoning is crucial:

After initial purchase: Before the first use, to build the foundation of your non-stick surface.

After thorough cleaning: Whenever you give your griddle a deep clean, stripping it back to the bare metal.

Monthly maintenance: A lighter seasoning once a month can help maintain that slick, protective layer.

Think of your griddle like a skilled pianist; regular practice keeps their skills sharp just as regular seasoning keeps your griddle in prime condition.

The How-To of Seasoning

Seasoning your Blackstone griddle isn't just necessary; it's surprisingly simple. Here's how you can ensure a perfectly seasoned griddle:

Clean Before Seasoning: Always start with a clean surface. Your griddle should be free from food debris and moisture. Lightly heat it to ensure it's completely dry.

Heat It Up: Fire up your griddle and set it to a high heat. This process will open up the pores of the metal, allowing the oil to penetrate deeply, which is crucial for a lasting season.

Apply Oil: Once your griddle is hot, apply a thin layer of high-smoke-point oil. Canola, flaxseed, or even grapeseed oil are excellent choices because of their ability to withstand high temperatures without breaking down. Spread the oil evenly across the surface using a paper towel or a high-heat resistant brush, covering every inch of the cooktop.

Smoke and Bake: Allow the oil to smoke and bake into the griddle. As the smoke wafts, it's a sign that the oil is bonding with the metal to create that coveted non-stick layer. Allow it to bake until the smoking stops, then repeat the oiling and baking process a few more times. Usually, three to four coats are sufficient for a robust initial seasoning.

Cool Down: After the final bake, let your griddle cool down naturally. This resting period solidifies the oil, cementing your seasoning efforts.

Aftercare: Post-seasoning, it's advisable to store your griddle in a cool, dry place. If outdoor elements are a concern, consider a griddle cover to protect it from moisture and debris.

Why Bother With Regular Seasoning?

You might wonder if frequent seasoning is overdoing it, but there's a good reason for this ritual. Regular seasoning develops the surface over time, enhancing its non-stick properties and ease of cooking while also minimizing sticking and rusting issues. This is especially vital after deep cleaning sessions where the griddle is scrubbed down to bare iron.

Moreover, flavor benefits are an undeniable boon. A well-seasoned griddle imparts a subtle, smoky flavor to foods, elevating simple recipes into memorable meals. Each seasoning session builds on this flavor foundation, enriching the tastes that transfer to your food.

9.3 Troubleshooting Common Issues

Here, we'll explore some common issues that new and seasoned griddle owners might face, along with straightforward solutions to keep your cooking adventures on track.

Uneven Heating: A Common Culprit

One of the frequent issues griddle users face is uneven heating. This can result in some parts of your food cooking faster than others, which is frustrating and can affect the quality of your meals. Typically, this problem arises from improper positioning of the griddle or accumulated grime affecting the burners.

Solution: Ensure your griddle is placed on a level surface. Regular maintenance and cleaning of the burners and the griddle surface can also prevent this issue. Refer to section 9.1 for detailed cleaning routines. If the problem persists, checking the burner's alignment and the regulator hose for any obstructions or kinks might be necessary.

Flare-Ups and Excessive Smoking

Flare-ups and excessive smoking can turn your cooking experience into less of a delight and more of a smoky nuisance, usually stemming from leftover food particles, excessive oil, or a buildup of grease.

Solution: Keep the griddle clean and scrape off any food residue or grease after each cooking session. Using less oil or switching to an oil with a higher smoke point—such as avocado oil instead of olive oil—can substantially reduce smoking. Regularly emptying the grease trap is also crucial in preventing flare-ups.

Rust Formation: The Griddle's Nemesis

Rust can quickly become a problem, especially if your griddle is exposed to the elements or left with moisture on its surface. It's disheartening to see your beautiful griddle marred by rust, but it's often easy to fix.

Solution: Prevention is your best defense. Always clean and thoroughly dry your griddle after use. Applying a light layer of oil after cleaning protects the surface from moisture. If rust appears, don't panic. Light rust can often be removed by heating the griddle, applying some oil, and scrubbing gently with a grill stone. After removing the rust, re-season your griddle to restore its protective coating.

Ignition Troubles

A griddle that won't ignite can put a damper on your cooking plans. Often, this is caused by issues with the ignition system or the propane connection.

Solution: First, ensure that the propane tank is connected properly and is not empty. Check the igniter battery if your model uses an electronic ignition system; it might need replacing. If manual ignition is required, a standard grill lighter can be used in the interim. Checking for any blockages in the burner orifices and cleaning them can also help to resolve ignition issues.

Inconsistent Temperature Control

Managing the griddle's temperature might seem challenging, especially for those new to griddle cooking. Temperature control is crucial for cooking meals evenly and to perfection.

Solution: Regularly monitor and adjust the temperature and be mindful of the wind, which can significantly impact the heat distribution. Investing in a wind guard can help stabilize the griddle's temperature. Also, getting to know the heat zones of your griddle can greatly enhance your control over cooking temperatures.

Sticky Food Despite Non-Stick Claims

Sometimes food sticks even to a well-seasoned griddle, which might be due to insufficient preheating or the quality of seasoning.

Solution: Always preheat the griddle properly before adding food. Ensure that the griddle is evenly seasoned. Sometimes adding a slight bit more oil to the cooking area before introducing food can prevent sticking.

Conclusion

While encountering issues with your Blackstone griddle might be disheartening, most problems have simple solutions. Regular maintenance, proper usage, and quickly addressing small issues as they arise can prevent them from becoming larger problems.

Each challenge offers an opportunity to better understand your griddle and improve your skill in handling it effectively.

9.4 Safety Precautions to Avoid Accidents

Safety, although not as enchanting as flipping that perfect pancake or searing a steak to excellence, is the foundation upon which every memorable cooking session stands. Adopting safety precautions not only averts accidents but ensures that every cooking experience remains joyful and stress-free.

Understanding Your Equipment

Familiarity with your Blackstone griddle goes beyond knowing how to whip up a gourmet meal. It includes understanding its components, operations, and, importantly, the safety features it offers. Each model comes with its unique set of instructions—heed them. Knowing how to properly ignite the griddle, adjust the temperature, and shut it down are basics that ensure safety and the longevity of your device.

Respect for Propane

For many, the use of propane is a new venture. Treat it with the respect it demands. Always check for leaks every time you connect the tank to your griddle. A simple soapy water test can reveal any escaping gas. If you find a leak, disconnect and do not attempt to use the griddle until the issue is resolved. Store propane tanks outside, upright, and away from direct sunlight. Remember, propane safety is not only about preventing fires but also about ensuring the wellbeing of everyone around the griddle.

The Right Place Matters

Location plays a pivotal role in safety. Your griddle should stand on a flat, stable surface to avoid it tipping over. Outdoors doesn't mean anywhere outdoors. Place it away from flammable materials, outdoor furniture, and, crucially, out of children's and pets' reach. The perimeter around your cooking area should be a designated safe zone, free from unnecessary foot traffic.

Dress for Success

Believe it or not, what you wear can impact your safety. Loose clothing can easily catch fire, so opt for tighter or well-fitted garments when manning the griddle. Additionally, consider wearing a heavy-duty apron to protect against splatters. Good quality, heat-resistant gloves can be a game-changer, offering protection and enhancing your grip when handling hot utensils or the griddle itself.

Mind the Heat

The allure of a sizzling griddle is undeniable, but never underestimate the heat it generates. Exercise caution when touching any part of the griddle. Use proper tools and utensils to avoid burns—long handles are your friends here, allowing you to flip and remove food safely. After cooking, give the griddle ample time to cool down before attempting to clean or cover it.

Cleaning and Maintenance: A Safety Pillar

Regular maintenance, including cleaning, is not solely about hygiene and performance but is a significant safety practice. Grease buildup can lead to fire hazards. Clean your griddle after each use, ensuring the removal of grease and food particles. Keeping the burners clear ensures they operate efficiently and safely.

Know How to React

Even with all precautions, unforeseen events can happen. Familiarize yourself with basic fire safety. If a grease fire occurs, never use water to douse it; this can lead to a dangerous flare-up. Instead, turn off the gas supply if you can safely reach it and use baking soda or a fire extinguisher designed for grease fires to smother the flames. Keeping a fire extinguisher nearby and knowing how to use it is wise.

Raising Awareness

If cooking is a family affair, educating everyone about safety is crucial. Children are naturally curious, and pets are unaware of dangers. Explain the risks and establish rules about keeping a safe distance from the griddle when it's in use. For additional peace of mind, consider barriers or physical markers to define the no-go zone around your cooking area.

Chapter 10:

Advanced Griddling Techniques

10.1 Layering Flavors

The Art of Building Flavor

Unlocking the full potential of your Blackstone griddle involves more than mastering the technical aspects of temperature control or griddle maintenance. It's about diving deep into the culinary world to understand how flavors work together, creating dishes that are a symphony of taste. Layering flavors is not just a technique; it's an art that transforms good meals into unforgettable dining experiences.

Starting with the Base

Every great dish starts with a foundation of flavor. This is usually achieved through the careful selection of ingredients that form the base of your meal. Onions, garlic, and spices sautéed at the beginning of your cooking process can set the stage for what's to come. But the base goes beyond what's thrown into the pan first; it's about understanding how these flavors will evolve with heat, how they will interact with main and secondary ingredients, and what role they will play in the final dish.

Building Complexity

As your dish progresses, think of each step as an opportunity to add a new layer. This can be achieved through seasoning, marinating, and the use of sauces and glazes. The key here is balance - knowing how much to add and when to add it, to prevent overpowering the dish while still contributing to the depth of flavor. For example, a marinated steak brings its own set of flavors to the griddle, which can be enhanced with a spice rub just before cooking, creating a complex, multi-dimensional taste.

The secret to building complexity is patience and precision. Layer flavors gradually, allowing each element to shine through without overshadowing the others.

Contrasts and Complements

An impactful way to add depth to your dishes is by introducing contrasting and complementary flavors. Contrasting flavors, like the acidity from a squeeze of lemon on a rich, griddled salmon, can elevate a dish by cutting through the heaviness and adding brightness. Complementary flavors, on the other hand, work together to enhance the overall taste. An example would be pairing the natural sweetness of grilled onions with the savory depth of a grilled burger.

Understanding the flavor profile of your ingredients and how they interact is crucial. This knowledge allows you to predict and manipulate the outcome, making the act of layering flavors a more controlled and intentional process.

Utilizing Freshness

Integrating fresh ingredients into your dishes adds a layer of freshness that can elevate the overall meal. Fresh herbs sprinkled over the finished dish, a dollop of vibrant, herby chimichurri on steak, or fresh citrus zest to brighten up a seafood platter are all examples of how freshness can be layered into your cooking. These elements offer a crisp contrast to the richness of griddled food, balancing the dish.

The Magic of Deglazing

Deglazing is not just a method of cleaning your griddle; it's a fantastic opportunity to introduce a new flavor layer. After griddling meats or vegetables, a fond - those browned bits left on the griddle - forms. By adding a liquid, such as wine, stock, or even water, and scraping these bits off, you create a concentrated sauce that can add incredible depth and richness to your dish.

Practice and Experimentation

Mastering the art of layering flavors requires practice and a willingness to experiment. The more you cook, the more intuitive these decisions become, enabling you to adjust and experiment with confidence. Start simple, gradually building your repertoire as you become more comfortable with how different flavors marry and transform under your careful orchestration.

Realize that not every experiment will be a success, and that's okay. Each attempt is a learning opportunity, bringing you one step closer to mastering the nuanced art of flavor layering.

In Conclusion

Layering flavors on your Blackstone griddle elevates cooking from a mere task to an exciting culinary adventure. By understanding the principles of building a flavor foundation, introducing complexity, balancing contrasts and complements, leveraging freshness, and utilizing deglazing techniques, you're equipped to create dishes that are not just meals but experiences.

10.2 Infusion and Experimentation

Embracing Innovation on Your Griddle

Infusion and experimentation play pivotal roles in transforming an ordinary griddle meal into an extraordinary culinary event. Here, we explore how to leverage infusion techniques and foster an experimental mindset to break the mold and discover new flavors.

Infusion: Revealing Deeper Flavors

Infusion is the process of incorporating deeper, more nuanced flavors into your food, often through the incorporation of herbs, spices, and other flavor agents. Unlike seasoning, which often sits on the surface, infusion ensures that these flavors permeate throughout your ingredients, enhancing their inherent qualities.

Infusing Oils and Butters

A fundamental technique to master is the infusion of oils and butters, which are used as the base for many griddled recipes. Begin by gently heating your choice of oil or butter on a low area of the griddle. Add robust flavors like minced garlic, rosemary, thyme, or chili flakes, allowing them to simmer. This gentle cooking process releases the flavors into the fats, creating an aromatic base that will carry through your entire dish.

Creating Marinades and Sauces

Marinades and sauces are perfect mediums for infusion. They combine acids, such as vinegars or citrus juices, with oils and seasonings, creating a flavorful solution that can tenderize and enhance your meats and vegetables. Consider a balsamic herb marinade for chicken, or a spicy lime and cilantro marinade for fish. The key is to allow your food ample time to marinate, ensuring that the flavors fully meld.

Experimentation: The Pathway to Personalization

Shifting from traditional uses of a griddle to more inventive applications can redefine your outdoor cooking experience. Encourage experimentation not only with ingredients but also in techniques.

Experimenting with Global Flavors

Your Blackreeze can be a portal to world cuisines. Experiment with global flavors by incorporating unique spices and ingredients from different cultures. Try making an authentic Japanese teppanyaki dinner or spice things up with some Mexican street tacos. Each cuisine offers distinctive elements that can expand your cooking repertoire and introduce your palette to new tastes.

Unconventional Ingredients

Who says you can only grill meats and vegetables? Challenge the norms by griddling ingredients that aren't traditionally cooked on a griddle. Try griddling slices of polenta or halloumi cheese, or even fruits like peaches and pineapples for a delightful caramelized outcome. Each new ingredient provides a learning opportunity and adds variety to your meals.

Integrating New Cooking Methods

Your griddling technique can evolve by integrating methods typically reserved for the kitchen stove. Try sautéing spices for a curry directly on the griddle or slow cooking a ragout sauce on a low heat corner while you grill vegetables on the other side. These methods allow you to multitask and make the most out of your griddle's versatile surface.

Learning from Each Experience

Each experimentation and infusion attempt provides invaluable insights, whether a resounding success or a learning curve. Take notes of what works and what doesn't, including how different flavors meld and react under griddle conditions. This practice not only refines your skills but also builds a personalized catalog of recipes and techniques that work best for your taste and style.

10.3 Expert Tips for Success

Understand Your Ingredients

The first and foremost tip is to truly understand your ingredients. Different foods interact uniquely with the griddle's surface. For example, delicate items like fish fillets require a different approach compared to more robust items like thick steak cuts. Recognizing the moisture content, natural sugars, and fat levels in your ingredients will guide you on how to manage them on the griddle. A steak with high-fat marbling will benefit from high heat that renders fat and creates a flavorful crust. In contrast, vegetables with high water content, such as zucchini or bell peppers, are best cooked over medium heat to evaporate moisture slowly, concentrating their flavors.

Manage Your Space

Efficiency on the Blackstone griddle isn't just about how you cook but also where you cook. Understand that your griddle offers a range of temperatures across its surface. Use the hotter zones for searing meats and the cooler areas to gently cook delicate items like vegetables or to keep already cooked foods warm. This strategic use of space not only prevents food from overcooking but also helps in timing your dishes to perfection, ensuring that everything comes off the griddle hot and ready to serve together.

The Art of Preheating

A sufficiently preheated griddle is crucial for achieving the best cooking results. A properly heated surface ensures that foods sear quickly, sealing in juices and creating a flavorful crust. Give your Blackstone griddle ample time to heat up, aiming for a surface temperature that suits your cooking needs. For searing meats, you'll want it hotter; for pancakes, a moderate heat is best. Use an infrared thermometer to precisely check the surface temperature and take the guesswork out of the equation.

Master the Flip

Turning or flipping your food at the right time is a skill that distinguishes the novices from the veterans in the world of griddling. A general rule is to only flip once—whether it's burgers, steaks, or pancakes. Wait until the food naturally releases from the griddle surface to flip it. This not only prevents sticking but also ensures a beautifully seared exterior. Use a long, sturdy spatula for flipping, providing you both control and distance from the hot griddle surface.

Use the Right Oils

The choice of oil can impact both the flavor of your food and your ability to cook at high temperatures without smoking out your backyard. High smoke point oils like avocado or canola are excellent for searing meats, while butter or olive oil can be used for lower temperature cooking, adding a rich flavor to vegetables and seafood. Experiment with infused oils to add an extra layer of taste to your dishes.

Keep It Clean

A clean griddle surface is non-negotiable for excellent cooking results. Food particles, old grease, and residue can not only affect the taste of your food but also impede its performance. Develop a habit of cleaning your griddle after each use. A hot water scrape while the griddle is still warm will make the task easier, followed by a light oiling to protect the surface until its next use.

Temperature Control is Key

The real secret to griddle mastery lies in managing the temperature. Unlike open grilling, the Blackstone griddle offers the advantage of precise temperature control. Learn to adjust the flame to react to what you're cooking. If you notice foods cooking too quickly on the outside while remaining raw inside, reduce the heat. Conversely, if you find the searing process too slow, don't be afraid to turn up the heat. Listening and watching how food responds on the griddle will be your best guide.

Incorporating these expert tips into your griddling practice will not only enhance your cooking experience but also ensure that every meal you prepare is a testament to your growing proficiency. Remember, mastering the Blackstone griddle is a process, one that rewards perseverance, curiosity, and a genuine love for cooking. So go forth and griddle with confidence, knowing that every step brings you closer to becoming the griddling enthusiast you aspire to be.

10.4 Secrets of Culinary Professionals

The Precision of Heat Control

One of the most crucial aspects that professionals emphasize is the mastery of heat control. Unlike the relative guesswork of conventional cooking methods, successful griddling hinges on your ability to manipulate heat precisely. This isn't just about setting your burner to high, medium, or low; it's about understanding the nuanced gradients of temperature across your griddle's surface and how these can be leveraged to produce the perfect sear on a steak or the gentle cook on a delicate piece of fish.

The Harmony of Flavors

Culinary professionals view their griddle not just as a cooking surface but as a canvas for flavor creation. The concept of building layers of flavor, a technique often revered and practiced in professional kitchens, is equally at home on the Blackstone Griddle. It starts with the seasoning of your griddle, followed by the choice of oils used for cooking, and extends to the judicious use of marinades, rubs, and finishing salts. Each step and ingredient adds a new depth of flavor, transforming simple ingredients into culinary masterpieces.

The Alchemy of Ingredients

A chef's palette of ingredients is vast and varied, and understanding the potential of each one when it comes to griddling can set you apart. Professionals know that the quality of ingredients can make or break a dish. This isn't just about choosing the freshest produce or the best cuts of meat; it's also about recognizing how different ingredients react under the griddle's intense heat. High moisture vegetables might need a different approach compared to starchy ones, and lean cuts of meat will cook differently than those marbled with fat. Selecting the right ingredient for the right dish and cooking method is a secret power in a chef's arsenal.

The Dynamics of Cooking

In a professional kitchen, timing is everything. This rings true for griddling as well. The sequence in which you add ingredients to the griddle can dramatically affect the outcome of your dish. Introducing ingredients at the right moment ensures that everything comes together in harmony, with each item perfectly cooked. This could mean starting with ingredients that take longer to cook before adding those that require a brief sear. It might also involve cooking at different temperatures, moving foods around the griddle to find their ideal cooking spot. This dynamic approach ensures each ingredient is respected and treated in a way that maximizes flavor.

The Craft of Presentation

Finally, culinary professionals understand that the visual presentation of a dish enhances the overall dining experience. This doesn't mean your griddled meals need to be plated with the precision of a Michelin-starred restaurant, but it does suggest a level of care and attention in how food is presented. Even on a griddle, aiming for those perfect sear marks on a steak or arranging vegetables in a visually appealing way can make the difference in how a meal is received.

Incorporating these secrets into your griddling practice requires patience, experimentation, and a bit of creativity. But don't be daunted. Each step you take brings you closer to the mastery that lies at the heart of professional culinary arts. Remember, the essence of griddling on a Blackstone isn't just in cooking foods but in creating experiences that gather friends and family around the table, sharing in the joy of delicious meals and the warmth of good company.

Chapter 11:

Seasonal and Occasional Cooking Ideas

11.1 Using Seasonal Produce

Using seasonal produce not only enhances the taste of your meals but also contributes to sustainability and supports local agriculture. Here, we explore how you can maximize the flavors of each season through thoughtful selection and preparation of ingredients on your griddle.

Harvesting the Seasons

The rhythm of nature dictates a diverse palette of flavors and textures available throughout the year. As a griddle enthusiast, aligning your cooking with this natural progression ensures that your dishes are both vibrant and nutritious.

Spring: Awakening Freshness

Spring brings a crisp, bright array of vegetables and fruits. Items like asparagus, snap peas, fresh greens, and early strawberries make their way into the markets. Imagine griddling asparagus with a light drizzle of olive oil and sea salt, achieving a delicious char that accentuates its earthy flavor. Pair these with grilled chicken or fish fillets marinated in lemon and herbs for a refreshing meal.

Summer: The Peak of Flavor

Summer offers an abundance of choices. Zucchini, bell peppers, corn, tomatoes, and berries come into their peak. Consider crafting a summer vegetable medley on your griddle, where the caramelization brings out the natural sugars in the corn and tomatoes, creating a sweet, robust flavor profile. Griddled peaches or pineapples can serve as a delightful dessert or a complement to grilled pork or seafood.

Autumn: Richness and Depth

As the air cools, autumn introduces heartier fare such as pumpkins, squashes, beets, and late apples. These ingredients are ideal for griddle roasting, which intensifies their inherent sweet and nutty flavors. Squash slices griddled with a touch of cinnamon and nutmeg can be a fantastic side dish or a base for a savory autumn hash.

Winter: Comfort and Celebration

Winter's produce may seem less varied but is no less flavorful. Root vegetables like carrots, parsnips, and potatoes thrive in cold weather and are perfect for griddling. Their dense texture and deep flavors develop wonderfully when cooked slowly on a low-heat section of your griddle, perhaps alongside a hearty cut of meat like steak or lamb chops.

Techniques for Seasonal Griddling

To truly honor the essence of each season's produce, certain griddling techniques can be employed to enhance their natural qualities.

Experimenting with Thickness and Slicing

The thickness and style of slicing your produce can affect how it absorbs heat and seasoning on the griddle. Thinly sliced zucchini cooks quickly and becomes slightly crispy, perfect for adding to a grilled sandwich or burger. In contrast, thicker slices of root vegetables can be par-cooked to maintain a tender, yet firm texture that holds up to robust seasoning.

Seasoning to Complement

Seasonal cooking benefits from a light hand with seasoning to allow the natural flavors to stand out. A simple combination of high-quality olive oil, salt, and freshly ground pepper often suffices. For a bolder taste, incorporate season-specific herbs like basil in summer or rosemary in winter.

Pairing with Proteins

Choosing the right protein to accompany your seasonal produce can turn a simple meal into a standout dish. Spring and summer vegetables pair beautifully with lighter proteins like chicken, fish, or tofu, all of which benefit from quick cooking on higher heat zones of your griddle. In contrast, the robust flavors of autumn and winter produce complement heartier proteins like beef or pork, which are enhanced by slower cooking on cooler sections.

Connecting with Your Community

One of the joys of seasonal eating is the connection it fosters with your local farming community. Frequenting farmer's markets or subscribing to a local CSA (Community Supported Agriculture) box not only supports local farmers but also inspires your menu as you discover the freshest ingredients available. This engagement enriches your culinary experience, providing stories of provenance and passion that you can share around the dinner table.

11.2 Griddle Cooking for Holidays and Special Events

Delving into the realm of holidays and special events on your Blackstone Griddle transforms ordinary backyard fare into feast-worthy extravaganzas. The beauty of these celebratory moments is that they afford the ultimate canvas for culinary creativity and the sharing of joyous tastes with loved ones under the open sky. Exquisite dining need not be confined to the indoors when you have a Blackstone Griddle at your service—a tool that beckons to imbue your gatherings with flame-kissed delight.

The Heart of Celebration: Planning Your Menu

When holidays roll around, there's anticipation in the air—a palpable excitement that's not just about the occasion but the people it brings together and the memories awaiting to be savored. Whether you're griddling for Thanksgiving, infusing Christmas with smoky tendrils of warmth, or sparking up the Fourth of July with sizzles and sparks, your Blackstone is your partner in culinary festivity.

Consider the holiday at hand, and allow traditions and seasonal flair to guide your menu planning. Thanksgiving might call for a twist on the classic with griddled turkey cutlets basted in herbed butter, while a Christmas gathering could glisten with succulent griddle-seared prime rib festooned with rosemary and garlic. The Fourth of July naturally leans towards a jubilant spread of burgers and grilled corn, but why not elevate it with gourmet toppings and an assortment of fresh, vibrant salsas?

Timing and Technique

With holidays often hosting a dance of dishes and a symphony of flavors, your Blackstone Griddle is the stage upon which you can use timing and technique to ensure a seamless performance. It's paramount to understand the interplay of quick-cooking items and those that require a slower finesse. Items like thinly sliced steak for fajitas or skewered shrimp will take their final bow quickly, receiving applause in the form of crisp edges and succulent centers.

For those dishes that favor a slow waltz, such as a thick brisket or robust portobello mushrooms, the cooler zones of your griddle await. Here, patience is your companion as you oversee their gentle transformation to tender delight—a process well-suited for conversation and a toast to the joys of the season, glass in hand as the sun dips low in the holiday sky.

The Elegance of Accompaniments: Sides and Desserts

A feast cannot subsist on main entrees alone; the accompaniments play a pivotal role in rounding out the banquet. Side dishes on a Blackstone Griddle can be as simple as grilled asparagus adorned with wisps of Parmesan or as indulgent as a mountain of caramelized onions and peppers destined to crown a sublime steak. Let's not forget that your griddle can host a bevy of desserts as well—think grilled peaches drizzled with a balsamic reduction or bananas foster, prepared al fresco for a dramatic dessert finale.

The Ties that Bind: Family and Tradition

As you griddle your way through the holidays and special events, remember that these moments are as much about forging connections as they are about the food. Your Blackstone Griddle is more than a cooking apparatus—it's a gathering point, a communal hearth where family traditions can simmer alongside those bell peppers, where stories are recounted as burger patties sizzle, and where laughter mingles with the enticing aroma of a holiday feast in the making.

The Mastery of Variables: Weather and Adaptability

Never underestimate the whims of weather when planning your outdoor holiday griddle cooking. The wise griddle master prepares for contingencies—a canny move allowing for adjustments on the fly should Mother Nature present a gusty challenge or an unexpected drizzle. Keep a close eye on the skies and plan accordingly to ensure that your al fresco culinary show goes on without a hitch.

11.3 Tailgating and Outdoor Party Recipes

As a Blackstone Griddle owner, you have the power to elevate these gatherings from simple pre-game fuel-ups to culinary events that rival the main attraction. With your griddle as the workhorse, you'll create dishes that bring fans together, turning a parking lot into an outdoor kitchen and a celebration of community and cuisine.

The Warm-Up: Prepping for the Big Game

Before the grill can take center stage, careful preparation sets you up for a tailgate triumph. Chopping vegetables, marinating meats, and assembling dry mixes at home will expedite your cooking process, allowing you to focus on the griddle's performance rather than mise en place. Remember, at a tailgate, you're not just serving food; you're also part of the revelry, so efficiency is key.

Always plan for more than the expected headcount. Tailgating is about generosity and impromptu invitations. Having extra servings ensures no one misses out and you might just make new friends as the mouthwatering scent of your cooking draws a crowd.

Touchdown-Worthy Main Events

Tailgating is synonymous with bold flavors and indulgent classics. Griddling provides the perfect opportunity to present those sought-after charred exteriors while keeping interiors juicy and tender. A Blackstone Griddle achieves this balance impeccably with burgers, hot dogs, and steaks earning their stripes over the consistent heat.

But why stop there? Imagine juicy chicken thighs glazed with a bourbon BBQ sauce, or skewers of marinated shrimp putting a coastal spin on your lineup. The versatility of the griddle allows you to venture into tacos filled with carne asada or even Philly cheesesteaks with onions and peppers melding together in a symphony of taste right before your eyes.

Sides That Steal the Show

Sides at a tailgate should never play second fiddle; they must be as satisfying and flavorsome as the main attraction. Think of grilled corn on the cob, brushed with melted butter and a sprinkle of chili powder for a bit of heat. Or maybe you envision a colorful array of bell peppers and onion petals becoming tender and sweet over the heat of your griddle, perfect to pile high beside a smoky, grilled sausage.

Potatoes also find a home at the tailgate—griddle-smashed and crisped to golden perfection or sliced into wedges and seasoned for a rustic take on fries. These accompaniments not only complement your proteins but can often become the unexpected hit of the party—easy to grab and munch on while debating the next play or discussing the season's highlights.

The Victory Lap: Drinks and Desserts

Post-game jubilation or consolation calls for a sweet finish and a refreshing beverage. Your griddle can handle both. Grilled fruit, such as pineapple slices or halved peaches, become caramelized delights with minimal effort. They can be served with a dollop of cream or taken to the next level with a sprinkle of cinnamon sugar and a quick flame kiss for a makeshift crème brûlée effect.

For drinks, the griddle can keep a pot of mulled cider warm, welcoming guests with a comforting hug of apple and spice. Or, it can serve as a surface for a large griddle-top pan where you can introduce guests to hot pancake batter cocktails—an inventive twist on serving a warming drink. Remember, these touches don't just cater to taste but also to experience, making your tailgate memorable.

Chapter 12:

Personalizing Your Griddle Experience

12.1 Customizing Your Griddle Setup

Creating a personalized setup for your Blackstone Griddle not only enhances your cooking experience but also aligns it uniquely with your lifestyle and culinary preferences. Let's embark on transforming your griddle into a more personalized cooking station, ensuring you maximize both its functionality and enjoyment.

Building Your Griddle Base

When you start personalizing your Blackstone Griddle setup, the first thing to consider is assembling a base that complements your specific needs. Whether you're in a backyard, on a camping trip, or tailgating, the versatility of your setup is crucial. You might choose a portable stand specifically designed for travel or a more permanent structure like a custom-built griddle station in your backyard. The key is stability and suitability for the environment in which you usually cook.

Enhancing Cooking Efficiency with Modifications

Modifying your griddle to suit your cooking methods can drastically improve your griddling efficiency. Consider adding hooks for easy access to grilling utensils or installing a side shelf for additional prep space. If you often griddle at night or in low-light conditions, attaching a magnetic LED light can provide much-needed illumination, making your cooking process smoother and safer.

Some enthusiasts even go as far as integrating a surround table attachment, which offers a substantial increase in work and serving space, allowing you to keep all your ingredients and tools within arm's reach. This is particularly beneficial when hosting larger groups, ensuring you stay organized and in control of the bustling griddle station.

Choosing Accessories That Complement Your Style

Selecting the right accessories not only boosts the utility of your griddle but also personalizes it. Start with essentials like a high-quality spatula, scraper, and basting cover. These tools are indispensable for a variety of recipes, whether you're flipping burgers or steaming vegetables.

From there, explore more specialized accessories tailored to your frequent dishes. For instance, if breakfast is your favorite meal to cook outdoors, a pancake dispenser or a bacon press could be perfect additions. For those who cherish a good stir-fry or taco night, consider a set of taco holders or a stainless steel chopper/scraper for handling vegetables and meats efficiently.

Protective Measures for Longevity

Taking care of your griddle is paramount, not just for maintenance, but also for extending its lifespan and performance. Start with a hardcover or soft cover; both provide protection against the elements, but your choice might differ depending on storage conditions and local weather patterns. For additional safety and to preserve the cooking surface, think about investing in a griddle mat to defend against spills and splatters.

For those living in harsh climates, consider the benefits of a full griddle enclosure or a customized protective shed. A cover not only prevents rusting and wear from exposure to moisture and debris but also keeps your griddle ready for use at a moment's notice, without the need for extensive cleaning or preparation beforehand.

Upgrading for Technological Convenience

In the modern grilling era, technology offers considerable advantages that can be integrated into your griddle setup. Digital thermometers, for instance, can help you maintain the perfect temperature, crucial for getting that ideal sear on a steak or cooking delicate foods like fish. Wireless versions can even alert you on your smartphone, allowing you to mingle with guests without neglecting the griddle. Advanced enthusiasts might consider smart griddles equipped with Wi-Fi or Bluetooth capabilities, enabling them to control temperature settings remotely and even receive notifications about their meal's progress. This integration of technology not only simplifies the cooking process but also adds a layer of fun and convenience that is hard to overlook.

Conclusion

As you tailor your Blackstone Griddle setup, keep in mind that each adjustment, accessory, and improvement should aim to enhance your cooking experience, reflect your personal style, and accommodate your culinary needs. By customizing your griddle environment wisely, you not only optimize your cooking sessions but also elevate the overall joy and satisfaction derived from griddling.

12.2 Accessorizing Your Space

Crafting the Griddle Ambiance

As a culinary enthusiast, your Blackstone Griddle is not just a cooking appliance—it's the heart of your outdoor culinary space. It's where flavors blossom and memories are seared alongside succulent steaks and vibrant veggies. To elevate this focal point of your gatherings, accessorizing the area surrounding your griddle is key. It's about creating an efficient, enjoyable, and personal cooking environment that invites you to explore and expand your culinary prowess.

A Harmonious Arrangement

The art of accessorizing your griddle space begins with a keen eye for balance and harmony. Start with a sleek, weather-resistant table to complement your griddle; this will serve as your mise en place, where spices, oils, and tools can be arranged for easy access. Opt for materials like stainless steel or finished wood, which not only withstand the elements but also add a touch of refinement to your outdoor kitchen.

Illuminating Your Craft

Lighting is a critical, yet often overlooked, accessory. A well-lit space transforms the act of cooking from routine to radiant—granted you don't overdo it. Strive for subtle, indirect lighting that illuminates without overwhelming. Consider solar-powered LED strings that create a soft ambiance, or, for more direct lighting, clamp-on grill lights provide focused illumination where you need it most.

Comfort in the Cooking Arena

Comfort is key when you're flipping burgers for the family or slow-cooking ribs to perfection. Treat yourself to an anti-fatigue mat where you stand, which will cushion your feet during those long grill sessions. Pair this with a griddle-side chair, so you can take a moment to sip your favorite beverage while supervising your simmering sauces and searing meats.

Sounds of Sizzle

The sizzle on your griddle should be accompanied by the sounds that inspire you. A weatherproof Bluetooth speaker that connects to your phone can fill the air with your favorite playlist, podcast, or the big game's live broadcast. Music not only motivates but also entertains your guests, creating a festive atmosphere around your culinary creations.

The Griddle Bar

Embrace the fusion of mixology and griddling by setting up a modest outdoor bar cart. Stock it with a few choice spirits, mixers, glasses, and an ice bucket. Having your bar cart within an arm's reach allows you to play the dual roles of chef and bartender, crafting cocktails that complement the dishes you serve.

Seasonal Decor that Whispers Elegance

Each season brings its own flavor, and adjusting your space's decor to match can enchant the senses. Opt for understated seasonal plants and flowers that don't distract from the culinary show but rather enhance the viewer's experience. In autumn, consider adding small pumpkins or corn husks, and in spring, brighten the area with a splash of seasonal florals.

A Touch of Green

Adding some potted herbs around your griddle space not only enhances your cooking with fresh flavors but also brings vibrant life to your outdoor kitchen. Choose herbs that you use frequently like basil, thyme, or rosemary. They'll be within reach as you cook, and their aromatic presence will invigorate both your dishes and the air around you.

Organizational Elegance

Organization is not just about practicality; it's a form of art. Invest in a magnetic strip or hooks for your utensils, keeping them orderly and at the ready. A stylish condiment rack or spice carousel can serve as functional decor, giving character to your space and rhythm to your cooking motions.

Setting the Table

Consider an adjacent area where guests can gather and watch the culinary magic happen. Equip this space with platters and serving utensils that match the aesthetic of your outdoor kitchen. Here, guests can mingle and feast their eyes on the sizzling delicacies before they indulge in the feast itself.

Weaving in Technology

A small, outdoor-safe screen can double as your digital cookbook and entertainment center. From streaming your favorite cooking channels for inspiration to displaying recipes, this tech accessory keeps your hands free and your mind filled with fresh ideas to transfer onto the griddle.

12.3 Sharing Your Creations on Social Media

Sharing your creations on platforms like Instagram, Facebook, or Pinterest connects you to a community that's ravenous for your next delectable post.

The Authentic Aesthetic: Crafting Your Shot

Crafting the perfect shot is not about adopting a professional photographer's stance; rather, it's about highlighting the raw beauty and authentic charm of your griddled masterpieces. The key is to seek natural lighting, capturing your dishes in the balmy glow of morning or the golden hue of a setting sun. This will unveil the textures and colors of your food in a way that built-in camera flashes can't. Showcase each sizzle mark, every vibrant veggie, and the steam rising off your latest creation, letting the food speak for itself.

The Narrative of Nourishment: Telling a Story

Your posts are more than mere visuals; they're narrations of your culinary journey. When captioning, let your passion for outdoor cooking spill into your words. Share a snippet of the challenge you faced flipping that hearty omelet or the triumph of a perfectly seared steak. Your followers will savor not just the imagery but the experience woven into your cooking tale.

Hashtags: The Condiments of Social Media

Consider hashtags as the spices of the social media realm. They amplify the flavor of your posts, making them searchable and savored by a broader audience. Use specific tags like #BlackstoneGriddleLove or broader ones such as #OutdoorCooking. They're your sous chefs in the digital kitchen, helping plate your content for the world to taste.

The Art of Engagement: Beyond Your Backyard

Social media isn't just a gallery; it's a bustling venue for interaction. Engage with your audience by asking questions like "What's your favorite griddle breakfast?" or "How do you achieve the perfect griddle sear?" Such prompts invite a feast of comments and can lead to discussions that enrich your skills and broaden your culinary horizon.

The Plate Less Traveled: Experimentation and Evolution

Encourage novelty in your outdoor griddle ecosystem by taking inspiration from the digital community and integrating what you learn into your grilling. Posting about your experimentation with new recipes or techniques inspires your followers to embark on their culinary adventures and often sparks a two-way exchange of insights.

Consistency: The Marinade of Social Presence

In the domain of social media, consistency is key. A steady stream of content keeps your followers engaged and looking forward to your next post. Approach your social channels as you would your griddle, with regular attention and a commitment to continual improvement.

Community Culinary Collabs: Cooking Up Connections

Collaborate with fellow griddle enthusiasts for joint cooking sessions or recipe exchanges. These partnerships not only broaden your reach but introduce fresh flavors and fusions to your repertoire, offering a potluck of ideas for you and your followers.

Sharing the Flip Side: The Challenges & Solutions

Your journey with the Blackstone Griddle may not always be a silky sauté. Share your challenges and the ways you've overcome them. Whether it was battling flare-ups or mastering temperature zones, your honesty helps demystify griddle cooking for beginners and showcases your growth as a griddle guru.

The Recipe Reveal: Building Anticipation

Tease upcoming content with snippets or "coming soon" posts. Sharing glimpses of ingredients or prep work can create anticipation for the full reveal, much like the savoring wait for a griddled dish to reach perfection.

The Proof in the Plate

Finally, let the results speak for themselves. Your mouthwatering dishes, once reserved for the dining table, now have a place at the global feast of social media.

Conclusion:

The Journey Ahead

As we draw the curtains on our comprehensive exploration of the Blackstone Griddle, let's take a moment to acknowledge that your journey with this versatile cooking companion is just beginning. Your griddle is now seasoned, not just by oil but by the experiences and memories you're about to create. With each meal, you'll sear more than just food; you'll sear stories into the soul of your outdoor kitchen, stories that will linger as long-lasting flavors in the hearts of those you cherish.

Embracing Mastery with Open Flames

You began this journey with perhaps a sprinkle of hesitance, a pinch of curiosity, and a tablespoon of excitement. Now, armed with newfound knowledge and skills, the control dials of your Blackstone Griddle transform into tools of empowerment. The grid surface is your canvas, and you, the brush-wielding artist, are ready to paint gastronomic masterpieces. From crackling breakfasts to twilight barbecues, every meal becomes a testament to your evolving mastery.

Overcoming the Initial Hurdles

It's natural to encounter some bumps in the road when embarking on a new venture. Perhaps the flames intimidated you, or the vastness of the griddle presented a daunting challenge. But remember, every skilled griddle chef was once a beginner, and each mistake is a lesson gleaming with the potential for growth. You've learned to trust your intuition, to adjust the heat as a reflection of your will, and to see the signs of readiness in your sizzling subjects. This understanding propels you beyond the fear of complexity into a realm of culinary confidence.

Reveling in the Simple Pleasures

Sometimes, it's the simplest dishes that bring us the greatest joys. A perfectly crisp-edged pancake, the aroma of griddled peppers, or a melt-in-your-mouth steak—these are the simple victories that accumulate into a rich cooking life. You've grasped techniques that transform humble ingredients into feats of flavor—essentials that will serve you in all culinary conditions.

The Future Seared with Friendship and Flavor

As you move ahead, remember that your Blackstone Griddle is a meeting place, a warm circle where friends and family gather in anticipation and leave with full bellies and full hearts. Anticipate laughter intermingling with the crackle of fats and oils, conversations deepening over the gentle hum of cooking, and bonds strengthening with each shared platter.

Continuing the Path of Culinary Exploration

There are infinite recipes to explore and endless skills to refine. Whether you find yourself curious about international cuisine or itching to tackle gourmet fare, the griddle's versatility is your gateway to exploration. Think of the rich, smoky veggies, spiced meats, or adventurous seafood waiting for your curious tongs to turn them.

The Griddle as a Lifestyle Companion

The resilience of your Blackstone Griddle makes it more than just a backyard ornament—it's a lifestyle companion, a witness to the changing seasons of both the year and your life. Its steadfast presence will offer comforting regularity, whether you're flipping burgers for the summer block party or crafting warm quesadillas on a brisk autumn evening.

The Legacy You Leave

Each time you cook, you're not just filling plates; you're creating tradition, passing down the touchstone of culinary love through your actions. Your griddle isn't simply a tool; it's a treasure trove of shared secrets and techniques that you'll pass on to eager hands in the years to come—becoming a part of your legacy.

In Service to Your Culinary Dreams

Ultimately, your Blackstone Griddle is in service to your culinary dreams. It's a springboard for the flavors you wish to create, the gatherings you aim to host, and the memories you aspire to build. Let it remind you that there are always new textures to produce, new palates to satisfy, and new culinary horizons to explore.

Made in the USA
Coppell, TX
04 October 2024

38176385R00059